Great Horses
of
The Past

Great Horses
of
The Past

By Bob Gray

Editor, HORSEMAN Magazine

CORDOVAN CORPORATION
HOUSTON   1967

Foreword

To readers unfamiliar with western horses, we should point out two things about this book. First, all the horses whose biographies appear here are stallions. Second, their breeding has been a major contributing factor to the Quarter Horse, Appaloosa or Paint breeds.

Those three breeds are what is meant by "western" horses. Western, in this case, does not mean west of the Mississippi River. It means horses which originated largely in the western states, to be sure, but horses which now are considered different in conformation, use and training from such breeds as the Standardbred, Tennessee Walker or Morgan.

Western horses, as they are now organized into breeds, are still relatively new in America. The Quarter Horse registry was formed in 1940 and began to spread all over the nation by the 1950s. In every state—as well as in Canada and Mexico—there are large Quarter Horse shows featuring contests which developed from early-day ranch work. They include cow cutting, calf roping, reining, barrel racing, and the horses carry riders in traditional stock saddles developed during the days of the old west.

The Appaloosa registry was formed in 1937 and it too began its major growth in the 1950s. The American Paint Horse Association, which is exclusively a western horse registry, was formed in 1962.

By contrast, the Thoroughbred breed registry—The Jockey Club—traces back to the 19th century and the Thoroughbred horse had its inception in England a century before that. Yet you will find repeated appearances of Thoroughbreds here because of the significant role they played in western breeding.

So what we seek to do in GREAT HORSES is present some of the best-known of the western breeds foundation sires that have passed from the scene. Most of these stallions had mixed blood—in some cases untraceable. Nearly all began life as racehorses or racing prospects. They usually raced at the shorter distances, thus the term "short horse." The match race, involving but two horses, was the particular delight of western frontier settlers in the middle and late 19th century. Often they raced for a quarter-mile and it was from this distance that the name Quarter Horse developed. There are references in equine history dating back to pre-colonial days that mention "Quarter Running Horses" but the Quarter Horse we know today is a direct descendant of animals owned and bred by the many ranches that helped settle the west and southwest.

At the risk of oversimplifying, it may be said that the western breeds developed from crossing blooded stock—Thoroughbreds, Morgans and Arabians—with native mustang-type mares that early ranchers rounded up on southwestern prairies after the Civil War. Nearly every ranch had its own breeding program. Generally, the ranchers would seek to find Thoroughbred-type stallions of substantial size, fifteen hands or taller, with great speed. Such studs would, when crossed on the small but tough mustang mares, produce a rather good cowhorse.

So it is not surprising that the early western sires were predominantly running horses. Speed was important to ranches handling cattle the same as to match race enthusiasts hoping to win a bundle from their neighbors.

The vast melting pot of western breeding programs—few of which kept detailed breeding records or pedigrees—took more than half a century to produce the sleek, magnificently-conformed western stock horses we have now. The fifteen stallions presented here don't begin to cover that gigantic process of evolution. Limitations of time and space prevented inclusion of some horses that should be represented. It is the author's hope—evidenced by our labeling this as Volume One —that future years will see more volumes in this series, including some that profile the lives and merit of the great mares and geldings that added so much to America's western horse lore.

Bob Gray
Houston, Texas
October, 1967

Acknowledgements

Much of this book is based on personal interviews conducted over a two year period, 1965-1967. Some of the interviews were done with the subjects in person, using a tape recorder. Most, however, were done by long distance telephone. And the author is glad that he doesn't really know what the bill for all that phoning totaled! It must have been considerable. Yet without Mister Bell's remarkable invention, this book could not have been written at all.

Nor would it have been possible without vital background fact and opinion from earlier writers and publications in this field. One primary reference for most of the chapters was the *Quarter Horse Journal,* published by The American Quarter Horse Association. Important too were the books and articles published over the past two decades by such writers and researchers as Ed Bateman, Bob Denhardt, Wayne Gard, Helen Michaelis, Nelson Nye, Franklin Reynolds and Darrell Sprott.

Doctor J. K. Northway of the King Ranch also assisted the author repeatedly in tracing pedigrees and providing expert opinion on bloodlines that go back to the early years of this century.

We also thank the following for important contributions of fact, recollection and, in some cases, old photographs:

The American Quarter Horse Association, The Appaloosa Horse Club, Inc., Lee Berry, George Blakeley, Jack Blasingame, Cletus Brown, Jr., Jack Casement, Roy Davis, Win DuBose, Sam Fancher, J. B. Ferguson, Lester Goodson, A. B. Green, Roy Hall, Billy Joe Hancock, Mr. and Mrs. Jess Hankins, Claude Hart, J. M. Huffington, George Humphreys, Mr. and Mrs. Byrne James, Ernest Lane, Wayne Laske, Owen E. Lay, F. Sonny LeBlanc, Lester J. Manning, Charlie McKnight, Max Michaelis, Carl Miles, George Ogle, Bill Peckham, Jay Pumphrey, Jack Randle, Jr., Bob Roberts, Bill Row, Hazel Hoffman Sanders, Mrs. Ethel Scott, Ella Moore Seale, Sam Ed Spence, Mike Stoner, Bob Sutherland, Manuel Benavides Volpe,

Mrs. Bea Wakeland, Bud Warren, Walt Wiggins, Tommy Young and Noah Zerringue.

Finally, and equally important, substantial work was invested in this book by Harold Holden, Jim Pitts, Tad and Mary Mizwa, Nell Gray and other members of the HORSEMAN Magazine staff. Their collective labor pains enabled the book to be foaled on schedule.

Contents

1

FLYING BOB

It was a long, slow fifteen mile walk from Abbeville, Louisiana, to Nunez, Louisiana, and Noah Zerringue was making this trip for the second time. The year was 1928, roads were rough and horse trailers were virtually unknown. To get a horse from one place to another you either rode or walked the animal. Noah didn't mind, though. This was a pleasure.

Behind his wagon walked the pride of Zerringue's life, a mare named Zerringue's Belle. She was no ordinary mare. Here was a racehorse and a champion. More, she was an investment in the future. Belle had brought fame, recognition and a fairly steady income to the Zerringue household. What more could a horse do for a man?

Now Belle was going to a stallion named Chicaro, owned by Bob Carter. He was standing at the farm of a retired Negro jockey named Paulenare Broussard. Early the previous year Noah had brought Belle to Chicaro for the first time. Nature, in her fickle way, had not seen fit to reward their union. Now Noah must try again. He desperately wanted a foal from Belle by Chicaro. He knew such an offspring could be nothing but a great short-distance running horse. In Cajun country, that's the name of the game.

Noah's confidence in Belle was well founded. Although some later pedigrees might show her as a daughter of Old D. J., one of the most respected Louisiana sires, we're told today that she was out of Walla by the Thoroughbred Dewey. But she was not a registered Thoroughbred herself.

Belle had a kind of peculiar saddle gait and some of Noah's neighbors did not think she could run. Not at first they didn't. Not until she started winning—and when she had won twenty-four match races, tied two and lost only one, there were no disbelievers left. Louisiana's racing fraternity— which seems to include nearly all of the male population— is traditionally ready to put its money where its mouth is, so Noah's neighbors aided greatly in his financial support during the late 1920s. There came a day, in fact, where he could hardly find a match race—and that's when Belle became a broodmare.

Chicaro wasn't exactly an unknown himself. Noah first saw the Thoroughbred horse at the Fairgrounds track in New Orleans in 1927—as the tote board showed Chicaro to be a 60–1 long shot. But Chicaro had done well on the eastern track and soon the odds dropped to 11–1. The stallion was still recovering from an operation to cure a throat infection, however, and his race that day suggested his running career might be over.

Impressed by Chicaro's ability nonetheless, Zerringue urged owner Carter to let the horse go to stud in the capable hands of the jockey, Broussard.

Noah's second trip to Chicaro was fruitful. Belle was in foal and on June 12, 1929, she gave birth to a strong bay colt. To show his appreciation to Bob Carter for having Chicaro within walking distance, Noah named the colt Bob. He was destined to become one of the great contributors of speed to Quarter Horses of future generations. But Bob's name wasn't yet complete.

He went into training before he was two and his early match races showed Bob would live up to his breeding. As a three-year-old, Bob was matched against a good colt belonging to Jack Hebert of Cecilia, Louisiana, for five arpents. In case "arpent" stumps you, that is the traditional distance measurement still in use among Louisiana running horsemen. It is 192 feet or sixty-four yards. Jack and Noah stood at the

This is one of the very few existing photos of Flying Bob and is said to have been taken in 1944 when he was fifteen years old and still a racehorse. Noah Zerringue is at the halter, the boy is thought to be the son of the unknown photographer who took the picture.

finish to see whose colt won. Jack's was favored—but Bob won with daylight between them. Stunned, Hebert wondered whether the colts had had an even start. For Bob to win, allowed Jack, "your colt had to be flying." The two men retired to the stands for refreshment—and then they talked to the starter. He confirmed an even start for the race. Bob had indeed been flying. And this resulted in the Zerringue colt's full name, Flying Bob. It was not long before Flying Bob was known to every horseman in the area. This meant that the son of Chicaro saw plenty of action—which in Louisiana meant a lot of cash on the line.

In fact, there are still tales told in the bayou country of Vermillion Parish about the size of the bets in the great series of races between Flying Bob and the fine mare, White Stocking. Owned by Gus Bergeron of C h u r c h Point, White Stocking was a noted daughter of the Thoroughbred sire, Doc Horn. Ironically, both Flying Bob and White Stocking had been in training under Bergeron's trainer Gabriel (Gob) Straus. Noah had been recovering from an operation and on his first trip back to the track, he heard Bergeron offering to match White Stocking against all comers at five arpents. Did that include Flying Bob? Noah asked. It did, replied Gus.

Several weeks later word spread through the countryside that the two horses would race at Church Point for a purse of $6,000. Flying Bob had his fans, so did White Stocking. Noah began to worry about the confidence all his friends had in Flying Bob.

"I knew that my boys had put up a lot of money," he told writer J. M. Huffington years later. "Money they had worked for in the sugar cane and rice fields. I had counseled them not to go too strong but many of them put up all they had. I never went to a race that I felt so humble or one that I wanted as bad to win."

On the day of the race a crowd began to gather at seven in the morning, according to one report, for a race scheduled at four in the afternoon. The tension and pressure were great as race time drew near and the tempo of the betting increased.

In those days, there were no electric starting gates for such match races in southern Louisiana. Every man held his own horse in the chutes until the starter yelled Go!

Flying Bob's rooters had an instant of horror as the starter yelled. Noah recalled in the Huffington account in 1951 that Bob dug in his front feet so hard that he lost his footing and started to his knees. "I thought the race was lost and as Bob came back up, leaping down his lane, I saw that White Stocking was in front and I knew that old Bob had to make that up and get ahead . . . as they went down the track I pondered every thrill and impulse of my emotions. I was excited, I wanted to win. The crowd was screaming and the thought of the $6,000 our boys had put up flashed in my mind.

"It just could not happen. It must not happen. Bob just had to win."

Within seconds the race was over and Noah hastened up the track and he could tell from the way the Flying Bob sup-

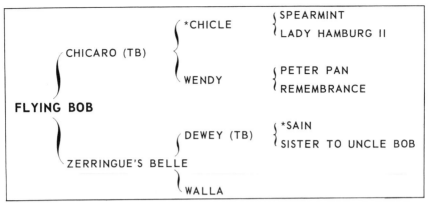

FLYING BOB

CHICARO (TB)
  *CHICLE
    SPEARMINT
    LADY HAMBURG II
  WENDY
    PETER PAN
    REMEMBRANCE

ZERRINGUE'S BELLE
  DEWEY (TB)
    *SAIN
    SISTER TO UNCLE BOB
  WALLA

porters were jumping up and down that his horse had won. It was one of his great moments of racing satisfaction.

But that was not the end of the Flying Bob-White Stocking rivalry. According to F. S. LeBlanc of Lafayette, a close friend of both Zerringue and Bergeron, the two great horses raced again—and again—a total of six times altogether. Flying Bob won three of the six, White Stocking won two and there was one tie. It was the distance that mattered, it finally developed. At four arpents, White Stocking had the edge. From five arpents on out to half a mile, Flying Bob was the winner.

Another Louisiana race mare that took Flying Bob's measure at the short distances was Black Annie. Her breeding went back to the immortal Louisiana running stud, Didier. He shows up as Old D. J. in pedigrees today—because of the way the Cajun dialect renders "Didier." Black Annie could negotiate the four-arpent distance in a fraction under thirteen seconds. And she beat Flying Bob at that distance. Nobody was more impressed by Bob, though, than Annie's owner, Joe Dugas of Lacasine, Louisiana. He could visualize what a colt by these two might be like—and so he bargained a bit with Noah.

Suggested Dugas: "We'll breed the mare. If the colt is a stud, he belongs to you and you pay me $200 when he is six months old. If it's a filly, the colt is mine and I owe you nothing." Done, agreed Noah and Black Annie was bred to Flying Bob. The foal, arriving in 1939, was named Bob, Jr. He was a superb combination of his parents' best qualities and at the age of four months, Joe was offered $500 for him by another party. But Dugas kept his word and sold Noah the colt at six months for the agreed-upon $200.

At eighteen months, Bob, Jr. went to the track and Noah started him in mechanical gates. Four men held stop watches on the colt as he raced two arpents. Sure enough, he was as fast as his sire and dam. And it was Bob, Jr., we are told, that was responsible for Flying Bob finally leaving his native Louisiana.

Noah Zerringue could see that Bob, Jr. could be a fine sire. But nobody was happier about it than the Randle family of Richmond, Texas. Vernon S. Randle and his son Jack had used up two cars, they told friends, driving back and forth to the Cajun country trying to get Noah to sell Flying Bob. He was tempted. After all, Flying Bob was nearly fifteen years old, as Noah studied the matter in the spring of 1944. The horse had sired somewhere in the neighborhood of seven hundred colts, it was estimated. There was no telling how much income Flying Bob had earned for Zerringue. Not just in money either. Times were hard in the 1930s and during breeding seasons Noah wouldn't wait for people to bring mares to him. Instead, he would hitch a trailer (one of the first horse trailers in southern Louisiana) to his car and haul the stud out through the bayou country. This way, Noah discovered, the horse could service several mares a day. Sometimes he got a $10 stud fee, sometimes he took farm produce in payment.

Now it was 1944 and Noah figured he could let the stallion go. Yet Flying Bob was still a racehorse, even at fifteen. He ran and won his last race the summer of 1944 against the Thoroughbred Boy Way in a race covering ten and one-half arpents at Mayo Romero's track near St. Martinville, Louisiana. Soon after, the Randles hauled Flying Bob to Texas. The purchase price, recalls Vernon S. (Jack) Randle, Jr., was $1,800. "We were looking for an outstanding stallion," he said, "and we thought Bob was the one to own."

Randle and his father (who died in the early 1950s), went together to buy Flying Bob. Randle describes the horse as standing about 14.3, weighing about 1,100. He was a dark bay with black mane and tail and black feet. There was a star in the stallion's face and a little streak of white down his nose, Randle remembers.

"I had seen him run twice and he won easily at a quarter of a mile," he said recently. "He did twenty-three (seconds)

Noah Zerringue of Erath, Louisiana, shown here at seventy, was one of the most active "short horse" men in the Cajun country. He got his first colt as a boy of eight, began shoeing racehorses as a young man and was soon breeding, training and racing. He assisted in collecting information on Flying Bob to record, for future horsemen, recollections of the most "talented" horse he ever owned.

in no trouble at all... I believe he ran longer distances on some of the Louisiana tracks under the name of Royal Bob."

Flying Bob's renown as a sire was already well established when he came to Texas. Since there was no Quarter Horse registry established until 1940, many of his colts in Louisiana were never registered. He was not registered as a Thoroughbred horse—at least not as Flying Bob—because his dam was not a registered Thoroughbred.

So when he came to Richmond, Texas, Randle tells us, Bob continued siring colts which were to become registered Quarter Horses. He calculates that Bob may have sired as many as four hundred Texas offspring in the two years before he died, in 1946. There are, however, no exact records—and if that number seems large it could be because the Randle breeding operation was one of the early ones to experiment with artificial breeding.

A young man at the time, Jack Randle—who is today a Baptist preacher at Center Point, Texas—studied all the information he could get about artificial insemination. "I guess we must have settled about forty per cent of the mares that way," he says. Flying Bob's stud fee then was $50.

Randle also says there has been some confusion over the years about "Bob Randle." This was the name of one of Flying Bob's colts. But none of Randle's family had the name. Vernon S., senior and junior, were the men who owned the horse.

Flying Bob's death at seventeen was unfortunate and premature. The stud was in perfect condition, Randle remembers, and was a calm, easy breeder. Then one day he got hold of some mouldy corn and that is what Randle thinks probably killed him.

Even though the horse was in his prime long before creation of a Quarter Horse registry, Flying Bob has left an impressive mark in the record books. Statistics at the American Quarter Horse Association show a total of sixty-one get of Flying Bob on record. As a sire of broodmares, he still ranks high in the Quarter Horse ranks. There are 165 grandget of Flying Bob recorded, through his daughters. He also ranks fourth among stallions from 1945 through 1965 who have seventeen or more daughters which have produced Register of Merit qualifiers. He had thirty-eight. And Flying Bob is still in fifth place for the same period for stallions whose daughters have produced thirty-one or more ROM qualifiers. His daughters have produced eighty-two.

So when you go to the short tracks these days, it is a safe bet that many of the quickest horses there will show Flying Bob somewhere in their pedigree. A couple of the top ten-rated racehorses in 1965 illustrate this. One was Bayou Bar out of Bayou Nell by Bob, Jr. by Flying Bob. Another was Joe Sherry by Joe Queen out of Queenie, a daughter of Bob.

These things doubtless are satisfying to the man who walked his mare those fifteen miles to Chicaro away back in '28. Noah Zerringue, you see, is still a racing fan and still lives in the Cajun country near Erath, Louisiana.

Zerringue keeps up his contacts with horsemen and with racing. He often is visited by young trainers, eager to hear his advice on short horses —and it is a reasonably safe bet that before the talk is done there will have been a few recollections of Flying Bob and those exciting days in the early 1930s when thousands of dollars rode the nose of a colt who has since become a storied name in Quarter Horse history.▲

2

HOLLYWOOD GOLD

In the life of every cowboy there is usually one horse that gets so close to him no other can take its place. Cowboys are not emotional about these things. Most maintain that they simply ride 'em as they come, the good with the bad. But in later years when they pause and look back, most oldtimers agree . . . yes, there was *one* special horse.

Sometimes it was because a particular horse was fast. Or smart. Or he could catch a calf. Hollywood Gold made his lasting impression because he was simply the best all-around ranch horse George Humphreys had ever seen. George and Hollywood Gold have got to be included in the same breath because they just naturally went together.

They got acquainted soon after the horse was foaled at one of the ranches that make up the Burnett Estate in north Texas. When Hollywood Gold was born, George had been with the ranch all his life. He was born in 1899 at a time when his father ran a chuck wagon for the founder of the 6666's, S. Burk Burnett. Young George signed on as a bronc rider at the age of fifteen for $30 a month—top wages at the time.

Anne Burnett Windfohr, (called "Miss Anne") granddaughter of old Burk, was owner by the time 1941 rolled around and George was manager.

On a visit to the Burnett's Triangle Ranch at Iowa Park, Texas, George caught sight of the best colt he'd ever seen.

"I liked him the very first time I saw him," he recalled later. And when he next saw Mrs. Windfohr, she asked him if he had seen anything he liked at Triangle.

"I sure did," he told her. "I saw a pretty little thing up in the lot . . . a little mouse-colored yearling stud colt."

"I know the one you mean," she replied. "As soon as he's old enough, I'm going to have Lige (Lige Reed, Triangle foreman) break him for me and take him to Fort Worth for my saddle horse."

George must have been clearly disappointed. Every time he saw his boss lady after that he asked about the stud colt. He made clear his opinion that the colt ought to make a good sire of cowhorses. But Miss Anne seemed to like the colt a lot so George had pretty well given up getting the youngster for a sire.

Then one day a year or so later, Humphreys came to ranch headquarters and there stood the colt—now a two-year-old. Miss Anne had sent word that the colt was Humphreys'.

"You liked him so well, I'm just going to give him to you," she told George later.

"I went to riding him easy before many months and he took right to it," Humphreys remembers. "When he was three, I bred him to a few mares, some by the ranch's studs . . . Tom, (Scooter) a remount stud we used named Buggins and also some sure enough good mares by King O'Neill II.

"The ranch had just bought some good mares in New Mexico that were part Thoroughbred. Hollywood's colts out of these mares the next spring sure looked good too. That was the first of more than twenty years of colts he was to produce."

No apologies need have been made at this time for Hollywood Gold's breeding but from the cowhorse-producing standpoint, the colt's sire and dam had not exactly set the world on fire. The sire was Gold Rush, a California stallion purchased by Anne Windfohr in the late 1930s. Gold Rush's grandsire on the top line was Del Rey, a Thoroughbred.

Hollywood Gold's mother, Triangle Lady 17, was one of the early registered Quarter Horses, with the registration

Hollywood Gold, in his prime, was used as an all-around ranch horse except during the breeding season when he was pasture bred to the 6666's mares. He took little part in major contest cuttings but was shown in exhibition by Humphreys. He transmitted his cow sense and ability to offspring to an extent equaled by few horses.

number of P-438. She had produced several colts by Gold Rush before Hollywood Gold was foaled. She was a big, buckskin Thoroughbred-type mare.

"Up until he came along," said George, "that combination had never produced anything worth a quarter. I guess they had saved it all up for him."

On a working cow ranch in the 1940s—long before the advent of the huge Quarter Horse show circuit of today—stallions worked as well as bred mares to earn their keep. So Hollywood Gold spent many of his early years under a saddle in cow work.

"I never showed him much," George related. "We had enough to do here without going to cuttings around the country, and there weren't as many then as now. I did take him to Stamford to the Old Cowboy's Reunion sometimes . . . I guess I'm a funny type of cowboy. I never was much for roping. Oh, I could catch a cow if I had to but I didn't do it when I could get out of it. But I could push or put one anywhere.

Old Hollywood, a son of Hollywood Gold, now is retired to stud at the 6666 Ranch, carrying on the bloodline. He is ridden here by Gayle Borland. Ranch officials note that the Hollywood Gold cross on Thoroughbred-type mares produced offspring with unusual cutting ability. Three of the six Hollywood Gold get that earned over $10,000 in cutting were out of Thoroughbred mares.

"Down at Stamford, Hollywood and I would give the folks a thrill by pushing a big Brahman bull out of the arena. Hollywood would just crowd up against that bull and put him right where he wanted him. The bull couldn't hook at him because they'd be shoulder to shoulder. Hollywood never hesitated a minute."

This, despite the fact that Hollywood Gold was not a big horse. Humphreys described him, fully grown, as standing 14.2 hands and weighing—in working condition—1,050 pounds. In his early years, the horse was bred by using traditional pasture-breeding procedures. He was turned out with perhaps two dozen mares at the beginning of each breeding season and he managed his own broodmare band. "He was one of the best herders I ever saw," said George in later years. "And he was seventeen or eighteen years old before

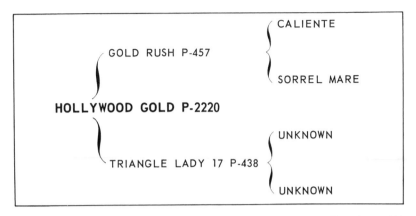

GOLD RUSH P-457
CALIENTE
SORREL MARE

HOLLYWOOD GOLD P-2220

TRIANGLE LADY 17 P-438
UNKNOWN
UNKNOWN

he had any trouble. Then he got a boogered knee. But he still settled some mares the last year he was alive.''

The years passed for the horse and his owner in workaday, unspectacular fashion. It soon began to be observed around the ranch that colts by Hollywood Gold exhibited his same interest in cattle. By now, it had come to be known as "cow sense" and you just didn't have a cutting horse if he didn't exhibit that quality.

Formation of the National Cutting Horse Association in 1946 followed by five years establishment of the American Quarter Horse Association. The AQHA registered horses while the NCHA was devoted solely to encouraging the sport of cow cutting. Soon names like Poco Bueno, Jessie James and Hollywood Gold were familiar to all who took the newly-organized sport seriously—and many in the stock saddle field did.

By the early 1960s, when cutting was on the verge of becoming a "big money" contest, the reputation of Hollywood Gold was secure. He never got any fancy training and he never won any of the big money, but his name was linked forever with the good cutting cowhorses. His descendants had seen to that.

They are so numerous and so famous today that, like the other prolific modern sires, to list a few is to overlook many. But the records compiled by the Burnett Estate in late 1966 tell an impressive story of how potent the Hollywood line became.

Hollywood Gold led all other stallions in the number of get to win more than $10,000 each in NCHA—approved cuttings: *Hollywood Lin,* 1964 World's Champion Cutting Horse, $41,512 in winnings; *Hollywood Cat,* $36,811; *Hollywood Snapper,* $21,462; *Mr. Gold 95,* $17,632; *Miss Holly Jo,* $11,847; and *Holly Reno,* $11,428. Since these figures were compiled in late 1966, monies won by these and other Hollywood Gold get have continued to spiral and in 1967 approached the quarter million dollar level.

Further, the old horse is the only Quarter Horse to have two of his get—Hollywood Lin and Hollywood Cat—in the NCHA Hall of Fame. He was also, in late 1966, ranked as the second leading Quarter Horse sire of performance working points with fifty-one of his get having earned 2,109 points. He had, to then, sired one AQHA Champion and thirty-five Register of Merit qualifiers.

Practically every month, when the national cutting horse group issues its current standings, Hollywood Gold is represented in the Top Ten standings with a son or daughter at or near the top.

Understandably, the horses of the various Burnett ranches are rich in Hollywood blood. For two decades his job was to produce working horses and good ones, at a time when hardly a cowboy on the place could envision a cowhorse becoming a show horse. And Hollywood earned his niche among great western stallions despite the fact that comparatively few of his offspring were ever shown. Most of his get, like the sire, spent their lives under a cowboy in a saddle. For his part, Hollywood Gold was active until his final years. He could still do an "honest job" of cutting a cow at the age of nineteen, said George Humphreys.

When writer Jane Pattie talked to George in late 1965, the grizzled ranchman missed his horse.

"Well," he told her, "we had to put the old horse to sleep last December. He was twenty-four years old and so crippled up that he couldn't get around. He's buried out there in front of the ranch house . . .

"There's a little mouse-colored stud colt . . . a pretty little thing . . . standing out in the lot right now," George added. "He's the last son of the old horse. He won't ever have to worry about having a home."▲

3

JOE HANCOCK

John Elbert "Bird" Ogle didn't know whether he was looking at a racehorse or a waste of time. He had agreed to train this colt . . . now he wasn't so sure.

It was a brown, rangy stud colt. The size was there. The length too. Yet Bird couldn't see a really good sprinter in that big-boned frame. And he sure did have about all the horses he could handle.

However, these people from Texas did raise some good ones. He shrugged. Oh, well. He had *said* he would, so he would.

And with that he told the Texan—Joe David Hancock—that it would cost him a dollar a day and that Hancock must furnish feed for the colt. Hancock agreed, then mounted up for the fifteen mile ride back to Nocona, Texas.

It could hardly be called an historic event, this perfunctory business of a rancher taking a colt from north Texas to Claypool, Oklahoma, for race training, in 1925. The Hancock family, already two generations deep in the horse business, raised cowhorses and an occasional racehorse. For his part, Ogle was one of the better-known running horse trainers of the period.

Yet the occasion was important. It was at Ogle's that the

colt was named for his owner, Joe Hancock. His arrival in Oklahoma would lead to prompt recognition, then fame, as a short-running sprinter. This would lead to later equine immortality as a sire of Quarter Horses.

Today there are professional horsemen who will insist that you are simply not well mounted unless your horse has some Joe Hancock blood in his pedigree. What's more, the Hancock fan club gains new adherents every year.

Nobody would have guessed any such thing that day when Bird Ogle first saw the big colt. Bird's son, George, remembers that his father didn't really want to fool with him because "he didn't think he could run."

That opinion did not last long.

"After he worked the horse a day or two with a mare," recalled George in 1967, "he beat the mare so bad that he thought something was wrong with the mare.

"When he took him to the Comanche (Oklahoma) Fair in a few weeks, he didn't much more than get him unloaded until a fellow jumped him up for a race. My brother, Doc, rode him against a big gray mare. This was the first race he ran. It was for $25 and was 250 yards and he won.

"In his second race, when they broke from the starting line, (the colt) broke so far ahead that the other man just paid the forfeit and called it quit."

Bird Ogle didn't need anybody to tell him, by this time, that he had a comer. This colt looked like he would win all the way from 250 clear out to three-eighths of a mile. And if you wanted to make money with horses in Oklahoma in the late 1920s, you had better have yourself a racehorse. That's where the green was.

Ogle and his sons raced mostly Thoroughbreds, since there was no Quarter Horse breed as such. But there was big money in match racing—horse against horse. Both owners and spectators wagered large sums and winners quickly gained wide reputations. It was as a match racehorse that the large brown colt gained almost instant success and well-deserved recognition.

This has been a source of wonder to many horsemen ever since. Genetically, some have argued, Joe Hancock had no

Joe Hancock.
V Ranch.

Most famous of the Joe Hancock photos that survive today is this one, thought to have been taken about 1928 when he was fully mature. Some horsemen felt that he lacked refinement, was too big-boned and rough in places. Certainly he would not win any halter classes today. But his size, speed and breeding became such important assets to his descendants that many ranchers and contestants are devoted Hancock enthusiasts.

business whatever being a racehorse. How could he be one? Look at his breeding:

He was twenty-five per cent Percheron!

It would be hard to convince any racehorse man today that an animal of draft horse breeding could ever be a successful sprinter. But the evidence is clear that Joe Hancock was one of the finest early-day "short" horses and at a remarkable variety of distances. He proved it in his brillant racing career and has proved it ever since through his progeny. We now know also that his breeding needs no apology from anybody.

The history of Joe Hancock should begin about 1921 with a traveling salesman who called at the ranch of John Jackson Hancock of Ochiltree County, in the Texas Panhandle. The

John Wilkins, Joe Hancock's sire, was well along in years when he sired Joe. This photo is thought to have been made about 1912. It shows that John Wilkins was used for ranch work, although his own sire, Peter McCue, was known primarily as a racehorse in the early days of this century. On his dam's side, John Wilkins was descended from some of the most famous Thoroughbred blood of the pre-Civil War period. Troubled with bad feet, John Wilkins did not race and spent much of his life on Charles Goodnight's JA Ranch.

peddler, according to John's grandson, Billy Joe, told the Hancocks about an old stallion that the JA Ranch was offering to sell. Horse named John Wilkins. Immediately the Hancocks were interested since most people of the period had heard of this noted son of Peter McCue, the famed Illinois racehorse— who today is considered one of the foundation sires of the Quarter Horse breed. John Wilkins was described as a dark bay with black mane and tail, some sixteen hands high and weighing about 1,300 pounds.

Troubled with bad feet all his life, the stallion never had a chance to demonstrate the speed his breeding should have provided. He was registered as a Thoroughbred and had spent most of his life as a sire at the JA spread, a ranch founded originally by Charles Goodnight, of trail driving and cow country fame. In time, the Hancocks corresponded with the JA Ranch and arranged to buy John Wilkins. John Hancock's son, Walter, then led him the one hundred miles back to Ochiltree County. At this time, the horse was perhaps fifteen years old.

John Wilkins' pedigree is worth considerable attention. His

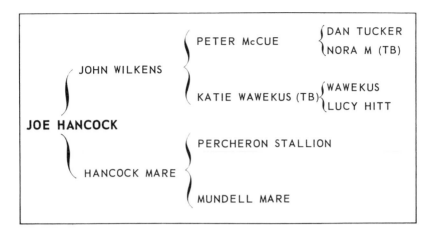

Pedigree chart:

- JOE HANCOCK
  - JOHN WILKENS
    - PETER McCUE
      - DAN TUCKER
      - NORA M (TB)
    - KATIE WAWEKUS (TB)
      - WAWEKUS
      - LUCY HITT
  - HANCOCK MARE
    - PERCHERON STALLION
    - MUNDELL MARE

sire, Peter McCue, had a monumental impact on the western horses of the early 20th century. One grandson, Old Sorrel of the King Ranch, founded an enormous dynasty in his own right. John Wilkins' dam, Katie Wawekus, was a product of Thoroughbred breeding at its best. A chestnut mare, she was foaled in 1888 in Illinois, not far from where Peter McCue was at stud. According to writer-historian Franklin Reynolds, Katie was by Wawekus by Alarm, he out of Maggie B. B. Maggie was by an Australian import that founded the American Fair Play line, which produced Man O'War. As for Alarm, he was considered one of the great sprinters produced in 19th century America and ran his best at anywhere from six furlongs to a mile. Katie Wawekus' dam was Lucy Hitt by Voltigeur. Interestingly, Voltigeur also sired Nora M., dam of Peter McCue.

On his dam's side, therefore, both grandam and grandsire of John Wilkins traced directly to the greatest Thoroughbreds, not only of the United States but of Great Britian.

So it was to produce well-bred horses that John Jackson Hancock purchased John Wilkins. Yet for his own reasons, now lost in time, Hancock at an earlier period had bred some of his best ranch mares to a black Percheron stallion. The draft horse was owned by Ralph Wilson, who lived about fifteen miles south of Perryton.

"I remember the Percheron well," Joe D. Hancock told Franklin Reynolds. "He was a solid black . . . a horse of splendid conformation, but not one of these extremely large Percherons that are sometimes seen. He was a horse of nice size for his purpose and I do recall he was a registered horse of pure blood."

One of the mares bred to the Percheron was known to the Hancock family as the Mundell mare. A man named John Mundell got her from a "traveling man," and the family records refer to her only as a "broke-down race mare." By the Percheron stud, she produced a good brown filly which the Hancocks kept as a broodmare. It was this filly which later became the mother of Joe Hancock.

J oe Hancock first saw daylight in the Texas Panhandle in 1923. As a yearling, the colt suffered a wire cut in the pasture—and it was this fact that brought him to the attention of young Joe D. Hancock. The cut and resulting treatment caused the colt to "gentle up" and the young man was soon bargaining with his father, John, to buy him.

"I knew . . . that I was going to have to own that colt," Hancock told Reynolds, "and that I'd never be happy until I did. I was there (at his father's house) about a week and kept that colt up and kept working with him every day. He was intelligent and he had a wonderful disposition.

"It so happened that when I had moved down here (to Nocona) I had left some horses at Father's place and before the week was out I had traded him two fillies for the colt. I knew that colt's breeding. I knew he was one-quarter Percheron but I also knew he was just exactly what I wanted . . ."

Not having any stallion shortage, it seemed reasonable in the following year to geld the young horse. Hancock called in the local veterinarian. It is to this unknown vet that Hancock later credited Joe Hancock remaining a stallion. The operation was ready to be performed when the vet advised the owner—in very plain language—that gelding a colt of Joe's obvious quality would be " . . . a great mistake and you'll regret it all the rest of your life."

That was good enough for owner Hancock and he immediately called off the operation and Joe Hancock remained a stallion. At this point, the horse had no real name. It was

When he was hauled as a young horse to his new home at Nocona, Texas, Joe Hancock rode in a 1927 model, borrowed stock trailer. When he got the horse to his destination, owner Hancock had to break down the trailer and ship it by rail back to where he had borrowed it. This photo was taken near the John Jackson Hancock Ranch, Perryton, Texas, and is from the Hancock family collection.

later, in Oklahoma, that the Ogles—not knowing what to call the colt—began calling him by his owner's name.

At this time, the horse's entire future was wrapped up in how quick he could get his nose under a finish wire. Racing then was horsedom's only money business and Joe was running for his share. The breeding potential that exists today for all good running stallions apparently did not then exist. During the years they had him, said George Ogle, Joe Hancock was only bred to two of their own mares.

One of Joe's most highly publicized victories came in 1928 at Oklahoma City when Joe was matched against a swift little Texas mare named Red Nell, owned by Bill Row.

"We matched a race for $1,000 on the side," remembers George. "This was for 250 yards . . . there were thousands of dollars bet that afternoon. The crowd looked like a big fair. . ."

George, at 120 pounds, was Joe's jockey. At the instant of the start, it didn't look good for Joe. According to Red Nell's owner, she jumped off to a good lead and it looked like she had Joe beat. Then at about 200 yards the big horse caught her and with a driving burst of speed whipped by the mare to win by half a length.

Joe Hancock - 1st
Skooter - 2d
Louis Pharr 3d
Time - 24⅓

Pawhuska - Okla
9-11-'30

This rare photo shows Joe Hancock winning a race at Pawhuska, Oklahoma, in 1930. Time recorded was 24.3 seconds. Race was probably a quarter-mile sprint. Note jockey easing up on stallion at finish pole. Apparently, Joe Hancock was not pushed to win this one. This may be the only existing photograph of Joe on the track.

In later years, Bill Row—Red Nell's owner—was to be one of the stallion's staunchest fans. At one time he bought two dozen Joe Hancock colts in one herd. "That horse had more action to be a heavy-boned horse than any I've ever seen," he told the writer in 1967.

After the race with Red Nell, Joe was "open to the world" for any distance up to three-eighths of a mile, and George Ogle recalls "they had it in the paper in Tulsa and everybody knew about it." By this time, of course, the Ogles were negotiating with his Texas owners to buy Joe Hancock. When the deal was made, George said that it cost $1,000 for them to own the stud. This was a tidy sum in the late 1920s but it was that caliber horse it took to whip all comers—then as now—in race-fevered Oklahoma.

Fully mature, Joe Hancock is described as a well-balanced animal standing about 15.3 and weighing some 1,300 pounds. His pictures suggest that he was too rough a horse in some respects to have anything approaching ideal stock horse conformation as we now applaud it. Yet, like many of the earlyday stallions, he consistently improved on himself through his offspring. In a letter to historian Bob Denhardt, the late Helen Michaelis said this:

"Some have said Joe Hancock was a freak. Had he been a freak. . . . he would not have been such a strong breeder of outstanding Quarter Horses. The Joe Hancocks have carried on for over thirty-five years on ranches, in the rodeo arena and on the race track. Whether one admires draft blood in his Quarter Horse or not, Joe Hancock's descendants look a lot more like Quarter Horses than some 15/16 Thoroughbreds of today that have been registered as Quarter Horses."

As it happened, Joe Hancock did become a Thoroughbred—for a brief time and on paper. Like such noted short racehorses as Peter McCue and Flying Bob, Joe Hancock was entered in the Thoroughbred stud book so that he could race on Thoroughbred tracks. Bob Denhardt wrote that Joe was registered as Brown Wool in the *American Stud Book*, Volume 14, Page 506. He was listed as having been foaled in 1925 by Wool Winder out of Maggie Murphy. Joe's life as a Thoroughbred lasted but a few years; when he matured, he no longer *looked* like a Thoroughbred. He finally retired to his own identity.

Aside from isolated match races, we have little documentary evidence of Joe's wins, times and earnings. Some reports have him running the quarter in just over twenty-two seconds, others say he never was defeated in a match race. No records were kept of such things in the 1920s and we will never know how many thousands of dollars the big brown stallion did actually earn. What is important is that his reputation swelled to such proportions that it was soon difficult to find competition, with money, to wager against him. But it was this reputation which anchored his future.

Joe Hancock might have retired to a relatively obscure life in the stud had it not been for a colorful Texas cowman named Tom L. Burnett. It was Tom's life-long dream to produce The World's Greatest Cowhorse. He had heard of the horse and had

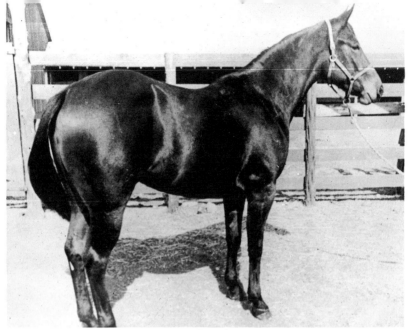

Anne Joe, a noted daughter of Joe Hancock, was one of seven off-spring from the great Burnett Ranch mare, Triangle Lady 7. Anne, in turn, produced twelve foals for the ranch, including both race horses and working horses. She lived until the age of twenty-two and some of Anne's daughters are still producing.

decided that Joe Hancock might be the stud to help him do it.

The Burnett name itself occupies a special place in western history. Burk Burnett was the pioneer cattleman who came to Texas before the Civil War, later founded the 6666 Ranch and was a giant name in Texas when cowboys still carried sixguns into town on Saturday night. Burnett's son, Tom, in 1905, started his own cattle operation in Texas, including the famed Triangle spread. Burnett's descendants still run the ranches, largely the way Burk and Tom put them together.

Tom Burnett was deeply concerned with upgrading the kind of cowhorse used on his vast ranges. He knew they needed more speed, more leg under them, more quality. It was said that he had "no use for a slow-witted cowboy or a slow horse." Apparently he wasn't much interested in racing but he did keep a sharp eye on the busy Oklahoma match race tracks for a possible foundation sire. And it is probable that Burnett knew of Peter McCue and John Wilkins. Both horses had been in Texas for breeding purposes. So when Joe Hancock was riding high in Oklahoma racing circles, negotiations commenced with the Ogle family. Burnett was willing to pay a good price for the famous southwestern grandson of Peter McCue. Yet he almost didn't get him.

Joe Tom (above) and Buck Hancock were the two Burnett Ranch
stallions selected to carry on the Hancock bloodline. Joe Tom was
considered the fastest son of the old horse. Sold to the Hepler
family of Arizona, Joe Tom was bought back after he won nine
races at Del Rio. Buck Hancock (below) was foaled in 1941 out of
Triangle Lady 40. Buck's daughters produced two AQHA Champions,
fourteen Register of Merit show horses and their get have earned
nearly 300 working points. Buck Hancock daughters also have produced such successful racehorses as Coe Badger 89 and Tonto's Jet.

Another of Joe Hancock's running daughters was Joan P-3246. She won twenty-one out of twenty-two match races in Texas and Oklahoma, later became a show mare, then a noted producer of show and running horses. Joan produced good colts by Chickamauga, Revenue and Coon Dog II, a son of Bert.

After much dickering, Bird Ogle finally agreed to sell the horse to the Texas cowman. George Ogle remembers that "Dad priced him on the phone—then began to regret it on the way down there."

But Ogle is described by his son as a man who stuck to the rules. In the horse business, once you price a horse, you sell him at that price. Period. It was still hard to part with Joe Hancock.

"Dad told me that he offered Burnett $200 (profit) if Burnett would let him take the horse home," said George. But a deal was a deal, Burnett insisted. The Oklahoman came home without the stud, richer by $2,000. This was an unheard-of price for a horse in the depression-ridden days of the early 1930s.

But it was one of Burnett's soundest investments. Joe Hancock's sons and daughters began populating the Burnett ranches—and do to this day. They have achieved recognition as conformation horses, in ranch work, in roping, in the other performance events—and yet many also have been racehorses. Principal sons of Joe Hancock used by the Burnett ranches included Joe Tom and Buck Hancock. Joe Tom, foaled in 1936, may have been Joe's fastest son. Sold to Elmer and Charles Hepler, he was raced with so much success that

Burnett's daughter, Anne Burnett Windfohr, bought him back for use as a sire.

When the American Quarter Horse Association was formed, Joe Hancock was issued the P-455 registration number. As of early 1964, wrote Denhardt in the *Quarter Horse Journal,* he had 107 registered get in the AQHA. This group included such horses as Little Joe the Wrangler, Red Man, Roan Hancock, Brown Joe, Little Black Joe, Tommy War Chief and Joan, as as well as the two earlier-named studs. Doubtless there were many earlier, unregistered offspring by Joe Hancock.

Joan may well be the most famous of Joe Hancock's known daughters. She mothered Steel Bars, Hot Heels, Joe Chick—and each of them in turn produced AAA or AA-rated running horses. Hot Heels' offspring included Mona Leta, Bob's Folly, Johnny Do It, and Mary Sunday, all AAA-rated. In the conformation area, Steel Bars was named the Honor Roll Halter Stallion of 1957. The get and produce of other Joe Hancock descendants is equally impressive and, most important, they run the gamut of performance, halter and racing excellance. Among rodeo veterans, the oldtimers very nearly remove their hats when Joe Hancock's name is mentioned. Go to practically any rodeo in the U. S. today, ask any calf or steer roper in sight how he likes his horses bred and the old stud's name is almost certain to be included.

Doctor Phil Smith of Abilene, one of the best-known veterinarians in the country, had an opportunity to observe Joe Hancock carefully and at close range. He did so, over a period of months, and in his words, Joe had "the strongest constitution and was the strongest breeding horse I ever saw."

Smith was called to treat the serious wire cut that Joe got on his left front foot. By the time treatment began, the cut was several days old and the screwworms were bad. The foot was cut nearly in two, Smith recalls, and on top of that the stud had seven broken ribs. "It would have killed a dozen other horses," he stated.

During the winter of 1942 the stallion was kept by Doctor Smith in Abilene where he could be treated daily. He was much improved by the time the 1943 breeding season began, so back he went to the Triangle Ranch. For several months, Smith traveled back and forth to check Joe's condition and the old horse was doing fine. But then in July, 1943, he foundered in his good front foot. He tried to walk on his other bad foot. It was no use. The horse could not stand. So at mid-afternoon, July 29, 1943, Joe Hancock was destroyed.

In 1943, prior to his final trouble, Doc Smith recalls Joe as standing above fifteen hands, weighing about 1,250 and being a sound breeder to the last.

It is probable that most experienced horsemen and Hancock enthusiasts think of Joe's blood as adding much to the bone and muscle of today's horses, as well as his speed. But among one particular group—the calf ropers—Hancock means something entirely different. Ironically, the horse that added new meaning to the word "go" is famous among many because of the way his descendants can stop. Veteran roper-trainer Jack Peek expressed the feelings of many ropers when he told a HORSEMAN Magazine writer in 1966 that a roping horse "has to have some Hancock in his breeding to suit me.

"There's no other horse that has a stop like a Hancock . . . They sit clear down in the dirt and stop . . . They just melt into the earth."▲

4

JOE REED P-3

Irritation gripped the handlers and the owner of the blazed-faced mare as they tried without success to connect the girth on her racing saddle.

It was too short. But it shouldn't have been. It fit her only a few months before. "I don't know what's wrong," growled the jockey, Will O'Neal. "I've never seen her like this. I can't get her to let that wind out. If I didn't know better, I'd say she was in foal."

Henry Lindsay, the owner, was equally annoyed. This mare was only thirty minutes away from a big money stakes race. A good crowd had gathered at the little track between Temple and Austin, Texas, and her opponent—the good running horse Dan Murphy—was fit and ready to cover the quarter mile distance. It was the fall of 1919 and one of the big recreational attractions in that day, as in later ones, was horse-to-horse short-distance racing.

Lindsay's mare was one of the greatest match racers of that era. Her name was Della Moore and she could fly. On this particular day, however, Della was not to run. Owner Lindsay knew something was wrong with his temperamental mare. He must have suspected that, somehow, she had gotten in foal.

So, the story goes, he called off the race—on the basis of it having rained that morning and the parties had agreed that if it did rain on race day, either side could cancel out. Lindsay then hurriedly got the mare examined and sure enough Della was expecting. Several months later, on January 7, 1920, she gave birth to an entirely unexpected and unwanted stud colt. He was destined to become one of the most famous animals in Quarter Horse history. His name was Joe Reed and he got off to a mighty rocky start.

Most people are not entirely sure just how Della Moore was bred to produce the colt. There are two popular versions, both interesting but both difficult to document these many decades later. Writing in *Famous Quarter Horse Sires,* Nelson Nye recalls the most familiar version: Seems that Della Moore was stabled next to the Thoroughbred stallion Joe Blair at a San Antonio race meet. One night, as the mare came into season, some stable hands in a crap game became annoyed at the commotion the mare and stallion made in their adjacent stalls. They achieved quiet at last by simply turning the stallion in with the mare, then resuming their more serious business with the dice.

The other version was recounted by Franklin Reynolds, writing in *The Quarter Horse Journal* in late 1959. He reported that a group of men leased Della Moore from Lindsay to run one match race—with a horse named Danger Boy. But on race day Della was in season, highly agitated and a fiery problem for her handlers. The other horse's owner—possibly worried that Della's condition might add speed to her feet—withdrew his horse. Disgusted, Della's backers figured one way to calm her down might be to let nature take its course. So they borrowed the stallion Joe Blair, bred the mare—then never did match her again. They also neglected, says Reynolds, to tell the owner about the mating when the mare went home.

At least these two stories do agree that Joe Blair *was* the daddy of Joe Reed. And they also make it clear that Owner Lindsay needed an unsolicited colt out of his highly successful race mare like he needed a hole in the head. In the early days of this century a good match racehorse, in the southwest, could sure help pay the rent and then some.

So it shouldn't have surprised anybody when Joe Reed saw

Joe Reed, shown here in his later years, is similar to some of the other early-day match racehorses. He does not exactly fit ideal conformation standards of the modern Quarter Horse. Yet his speed and breeding were important ingredients in the evolutionary process by which the breed became what it is.

the last of his momma a couple of months after his arrival. He then had to get along on cow's milk and some mash, finally was turned out to make it in the pasture on his own. Della Moore went back into race training.

The new arrival actually had two strikes on him. Not only was he unwanted, he wasn't much to look at either. It is possible too that the late Mr. Lindsay did not find out for some time that a highly-respected stallion like Joe Blair was the sire of the colt. If Della Moore hadn't been the momma, the youngster probably would have been given away to face an anonymous future as a gelding.

But this *was* Della's youngster, so when he was finally put into race training young Joe Reed at least still remained a stallion. His pictures then show him to be anything but a stud prospect, however. Particularly from the front he appeared

Della Moore, Joe Reed's great racing mother, was in her running prime when she turned up in foal—much to the irritation of her owner. Della was only a few minutes away from a match race when her pregnancy was discovered. When Joe Reed was foaled he was unwanted and soon taken off his dam so she could go back to racing.

narrow-chested with little of that "V" you look for nowadays in your stallion candidates. But at some point in his early life he began to get his share of the groceries. As a full-grown horse he appeared to have been well filled-out and, while no halter winner by modern standards, nobody needed to apologize for Joe Reed's looks.

As for Joe's racing career, here again we find disagreement among the writers of past years. Reynolds in his *Quarter Horse Journal* writings suggests that Joe Reed "launched on a most successful career of quarter-racing."

In contrast, Veteran Quarter Horse man Bob Denhardt, writing in the *Journal's* July 1963, issue, comments: "Joe Reed, never made the name for himself on the tracks he should have so we have no records or famous match races to talk about."

It is reported that Joe Reed was tried and clocked at the short distances and ran well. The story is popular that Lindsay took the colt north as a two-year-old and raised a flock of eyebrows at one track when he asked that Joe Reed be timed at one-sixteenth of a mile. Although Lindsay had fed Joe well the preceding winter, the colt must still have looked pretty

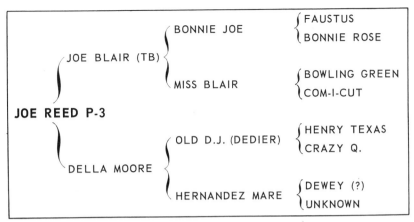

		FAUSTUS
JOE BLAIR (TB)	BONNIE JOE	BONNIE ROSE
	MISS BLAIR	BOWLING GREEN
		COM-I-CUT

JOE REED P-3

	OLD D.J. (DEDIER)	HENRY TEXAS
		CRAZY Q.
DELLA MOORE	HERNANDEZ MARE	DEWEY (?)
		UNKNOWN

poor as a running prospect, particularly a sprinter.

However, the timers got out their watches and Joe Reed took off. As he flashed across the line and the watches snapped, the timers were astonished. The time was 5.4 seconds. It developed that Joe, although a good sprinter, could not hold up with the Thoroughbreds at the longer distances. Nelson Nye says he did run a half-mile in forty-seven flat but it appeared that Joe's best distance was the quarter mile. He is said to have covered the four-forty in twenty-two seconds—and one of his later owners claimed that both of Joe Reed's parents did the same.

One obvious problem facing the colt at that time was that the Quarter Horse breed, as such, did not exist in the early 1920s. (The registry was not formed until 1940.) The established tracks raced registered Thoroughbred horses. Only in the short distance match races did unregistered, cross-bred or unknown-pedigree horses stand much chance of recognition.

And that's where Joe Reed lost out. His daddy was a registered Thoroughbred. His mother was an acknowledged short-distance champion—but she was not a registered mare. His owner, Lindsay, was primarily in the Thoroughbred running horse business, by all accounts, so that meant Joe Reed actually had a limited future in his stable.

For the pedigree-minded, however, the colt's parents had had some impressive ancestors.

His sire, Joe Blair, was a Jockey Club Thoroughbred that had burned up some of the Arizona tracks in short distance races. At Juarez, Mexico, reports Bob Denhardt, Joe Blair lost a tough race to the great Pan Zareta mare, but she had to set a new world's record for three and one-half furlongs to win it.

He ran that distance himself in thirty-nine seconds. Joe Blair was by Bonnie Joe out of Miss Blair. Bonnie Joe was by Faustus and the extended pedigree shows Faustus by Enquirer by Leamington. Here was the kind of Thoroughbred horse that the early "short horse" men wanted for their quick little mares—the kind that had that early speed with the size and bottom to go with it.

For her part, Della Moore's place in Quarter Horse history is secure. Besides Joe Reed, she also produced Joe Moore and Grano de Oro. Foaled near Scott, Louisiana, she was bred and owned by Ludovic Stemmans, a farmer by vocation but a racehorse man most all the time. He also raised and raced Della Moore's mother, an Hernandez mare thought to be by the Thoroughbred, Dewey. When the mare had so thoroughly established herself as the local champ that it was hard to find competition, Stemmans decided it was time for her to produce another racehorse. As a mate for her, he picked a stallion named Dedier. As the Cajuns of Louisiana pronounce that name, it comes out "D.J." So the horse eventually came to be called Old D.J. The union produced Della Moore—and she was no accident. Dedier went on to become a great sire of broodmares. Some of his daughters produced such horses as Texas Boy, Babe Ruth, Danger Boy and Mae West.

After a money-winning career on Louisiana short tracks, Della Moore was purchased by Boyd Simar and brought to Texas. It was there that Henry Lindsay, the Granger, Texas, rancher became her owner. Della Moore finally ended her distinguished career at the breeding farm of Ott Adams in Alfred, Texas, where her descendants through Joe Moore established still another dynasty.

By 1924, Lindsay had apparently satisfied himself that Joe Reed was not to achieve greatness as a running horse. He sold the young horse that year to one of the best-known and colorful men then at the short tracks, J. W. House of Cameron, Texas. It was House who established Joe Reed's place in western horse history as a great sire. And the colt that helped him do that arrived in 1936, when "Joe Reed breeding" was already widely recognized in Texas. The youngster that put his sire in all the Quarter record books was Joe Reed II, bred by House, from the half-Thoroughbred mare, Nellene. She

34

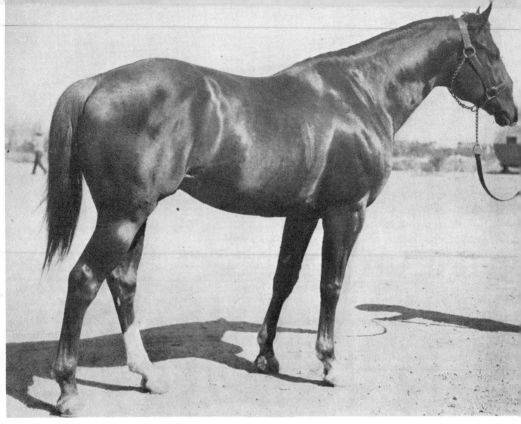

Joe Reed II may well be the best-known son of Joe Reed. Bred by John M. House, he was owned for many years by Bert Woods of Tucson, Arizona. Joe Reed II won many races during his career and ranked high in his siring of Register of Merit running colts.

was by Fleeting Time (TB) by High Time by Ultimus. Her mother was Little Red Nell, a direct descendant of Traveler through Texas Chief.

The story of Joe Reed II is a dramatic story in itself, of a horse that enjoyed a brief and painful but magnificent racing career. Yet in the record books, this stallion's great contribution to the breed is found through his breeding. His son, Leo, stands today as one of the foremost sires in several categories. Leo was the leading maternal grandsire of Register of Merit qualifiers, from 1945 through 1965. He ranked second to Three Bars as a leading sire of ROM qualifiers for that same period.

Despite the lapse in years, Joe Reed breeding is still well represented in the list of current leading sires of race winners. In the 1965 totals, Joak by Joe Reed II was seventeenth on the list with sixteen winners, winning forty-one races. Leo and two of Leo's sons are prominent in the same list—making it clear that, even in competition with such modern Thoroughbred sires as Top Deck and Three Bars, Joe Reed breeding continues to produce successful racehorses. What's more, they're horses with eye appeal. You won't go to a major Quarter Horse show without finding some Joe Reed-bred horses prominent in the halter classes.

During the 1930s, Joe Reed enjoyed a wide reputation as a sire and his owner bred him to many outside mares. In 1938 his fame had spread to other states and Dr. J. J. Slankard of Elk City, Oklahoma, began negotiations to buy the stallion. The deal was completed finally and Joe Reed moved to what was to be his final home. It was in Elk City that Bob Denhardt —who was to be one of the driving forces in establishment of the Quarter Horse breed—saw Joe Reed and left us this vivid word picture:

". . . Old Joe's front legs were not set too wide apart. While they did not come out the same hole, they were a little too close together. His legs were better than Leo's, being cleaner with somewhat flatter bone. He also had four white feet, with considerable more white than Leo. Both Joe Reed II, Leo's sire, and Leo, had better heads than Old Joe. Old Joe's head was a little plain. He did have, however, the neatest, and most alert little fox ears you'll ever see on a horse. Old Joe stood on a little too much leg to please a dyed-in-the-wool Quarter Horse fan, but just right for a Thoroughbred fan. It is difficult to fault him much more, when you realize that as a baby he had almost no care. He reminded me of what Coke Blake once said when describing a horse to me — he had 'the eye of an eagle and the step of a deer.' "

Denhardt added that he "chinned" the horse and estimated him to be almost 15.2 and his weight at pretty close to 1,050 pounds.

At the time that Denhardt wrote of Joe Reed, the horse was second ranking progenitor in numbers of horses registered in the American Quarter Horse Association. It was understandable that he would be assigned to the P-3 position in assigning numbers to foundation sires of the breed.

Old Joe remained active as a breeding horse throughout a long life. He died of a heart attack, after breeding a mare, on May 19, 1947. He was twenty-seven years old and his descendants already had installed him among the Quarter Horse immortals. ▲

5

JOKER B.

July 21, 1941, could have been a day of some celebration at the Casement ranch in northern Colorado. The good blue roan mare the Casements had bought from veteran Quarter Horse breeder Coke Roberds was due to foal. She was carrying the service of the Casement's fine stud, Red Dog—P-55 in the new Quarter Horse stud book.

The dam, Blue Vitriol, delivered her foal some ten miles north of Steamboat Springs, along the Elk River. But as Jack Casement recalls it, there was no cause for celebration.

The mare produced a spotted colt. The Casements were in the Quarter Horse business — and spots weren't, and still aren't, a welcome addition to that business.

"We were certainly expecting a solid-colored colt," says Jack. So when Blue Vitriol's offspring turned up wearing a loud blanket across his hips, he got a restrained reception. A family noted for helping found the Quarter Horse breed had an Appaloosa on its hands and, added Casement, with some understatement, "This was not too desirable."

Despite this lukewarm welcome, the spotted stud colt had a lot going for him. His conformation, for one thing, was excellent. "A real nice-looking colt," Casement agreed after looking the foal over.

Another thing was his pedigree. A weanling almost couldn't pick better ancestors. His sire, Red Dog, was by Balley Mooney by Concho Colonel. And it was Concho Colonel, obtained by Dan Casement—Jack's father—that helped put the Casements in the horse business. He had come from the legendary English horseman, Billy Anson. Red Dog's dam was Cinnabar by Old Joe of New Mexico by Harmon Baker.

On the dam's side, Blue Vitriol was by Brown Dick by the Thoroughbred Deering Doe by Desmont by St. Simon. From Blue Vitriol's side, says Casement, came the Appaloosa influence. Leopard was her dam by the great Old Fred, and she was out of a Primero mare. And that mare apparently carried the spotted genes transmitted through Leopard and Blue Vitriol.

Modern breeders have tremendous respect for the top and bottom of this pedigree. Some—like the Casements and Hank Wiescamp—have built their entire breeding programs around Red Dog and Old Fred blood.

Another thing the colt had going for him was the moment in history he arrived. The infant Appaloosa breed was beginning to attract attention and some horsemen sensed that the spotted horses had a future. This particular colt certainly did.

He was later to be known as Joker B. And the time would come when his owner could say with justification that he was the most famous Appaloosa in the world.

But in 1941 he was just another good colt in a Colorado pasture full of good colts. And he stayed at the Casement ranch only about six months. During that time Jack gave the colt to his wife, Xenia. They had recently moved from southern to northern Colorado and were pleased to have REA electricity in their new home. But they had no electrical appliances.

They did have a neighbor, Jack Blasingame, who liked the spotted foal and it didn't take long for a deal to be made. Jack Casement was pleased to see his wife get enough for the colt to buy herself a vacuum cleaner. Blasingame recalls the purchase price as $250.

He says that when he picked up the colt from the Casements it did not have a name. He admired the youngster's breeding and size. And he soon had a buyer. Blasingame kept the spotted colt only about two weeks before selling it to the late Bob Cantrall of Reno, Nevada. The $750 selling price

This is the widely-printed photograph of Joker B. most often seen in recent years. It is a picture which tells much about the horse's breeding. The well-muscled forearm and gaskin, depth of heart and overall athletic look have meaning for those familiar with Coke Roberds-Casement breeding. More than 500 copies of this photo are said to be hanging in motels and restaurants throughout the U. S.

was much money in those days, Jack remembers, and he was mighty glad to take that $500 profit.

Cantrall may have been the only owner who did not make money from owning Joker B. He too apparently kept the colt only a short time since Tommy Young of Las Vegas, Nevada, recalls buying him in March, 1942, when young Joker was not yet a full year old. Young says his purchase price was $400.

Up to this point, the colt's owners were impressed by several qualities in him, besides his conformation. One was the color. Joker B. apparently started life off with a dark blue roan appearance to his forward body and neck, with the loud blanket over his hips. That is how Young recalls him in 1942 when he was a yearling.

Speed was part of the Joker B. stock-in-trade and he gained fame on the rodeo circuit—first for his ability to catch a calf or a steer. Later, he was used for barrel and stake racing and it was not until comparatively late in life (above) that he demonstrated his speed at the race track. As an eight-year-old, Joker B. was registered in the American Quarter Racing Association. The horse was still winning races at the comparatively old age of thirteen.

Another characteristic was the colt's docility. He was, in fact, a little on the lazy side and, as a result, an easy stallion to live with all his life. Young started the colt off with both a name and some training.

"They called him 'Domino' when I got him," says Young, but Tommy once had to ride a horse named Domino he didn't like. So for reasons he cannot now recall, Young picked the name Joker. The "B" was to come years later.

Young broke and started Joker at about two years of age. He was "no trouble" at all and soon the young stud was familiar with rodeos and cow work. Eventually, he was to be used as a roping horse, for bulldogging, hazing, to pick up broncs and for general cow handling.

At the time Young bought Joker, there was still relatively little market for Appaloosas and it never seemed reasonable to charge a stud fee for breeding Joker. He did it free for friends and neighbors who wanted a mare bred to the stallion.

"When I bought him, you could buy spotted horses for $100 a carload," Young told the writer. And if anybody wanted to try and produce more spotted horses from Joker, he was glad

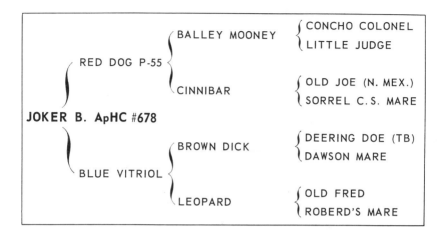

RED DOG P-55

BALLEY MOONEY
- CONCHO COLONEL
- LITTLE JUDGE

CINNIBAR
- OLD JOE (N. MEX.)
- SORREL C.S. MARE

JOKER B. ApHC #678

BLUE VITRIOL

BROWN DICK
- DEERING DOE (TB)
- DAWSON MARE

LEOPARD
- OLD FRED
- ROBERD'S MARE

to oblige. As far as he was concerned, Joker was a utility and contest animal.

While Young had the stallion, Joker got off to a rocky start as a producer of spotted colts. First mare he was bred to, says Young, was a little bay mare owned by Slats Jacobs, an old time bulldogger. The foal was not spotted. Over a period of four years, in fact, *Joker did not produce a single spotted foal* from any of the mares he was bred to, Young says.

No one could have then suspected that the young stallion would one day be considered the leading producer of spotted Appaloosa champions of the country. At this time also, Joker was not considered as fiery a stallion as some of the cowboys would have wished, Sam Fancher included.

Sam, father of noted barrel racer Sammy Fancher Thurman, was on the rodeo circuit in the mid-1940s. When his roping horse got hurt, Sam borrowed Joker from Tommy Young to use for the summer. A bulldogger as well as roper, Sam remembers Joker as ". . . thick-hided and awful lazy. You couldn't get a lot out of him unless you really went to work on him. Sometimes I'd have to take him out behind the chute and tune him up. Then he could really run."

One thing Fancher remembers he sure did like to do on Joker was to pick up broncs after the whistle blew. "I'll tell you, that horse (Joker) could catch those horses." And by the end of the summer Fancher says he was placing well on the stallion. Fully-grown at that time, Joker weighed 1,200 pounds and stood about fifteen hands.

In 1946, Joker changed owners again. Lee Berry of Barstow, California, went to breed a mare to Joker, took a second look, then a third. "He was a deep blue in front—looked like somebody had poured water on him. And of course I had to ride him a little. Boy, what a front end. And what a rear end. Any way you looked at him, he looked real good."

When Berry went to pick up the mare he saw the stud again, then started home.

"The farther I drove down the road toward home, the more I wanted to turn around and go back after him. Couldn't stand it any longer. I found an old corral near the highway and unloaded the mare and hit for the ranch where Tommy was working..."

The upshot was that Berry soon owned the stud. Young recalls the purchase price as $1,500. But there was a sense of loss to him. Berry says Tommy didn't eat his dinner that night. "Some horses come only once in a lifetime and that's the kind of horse Joker was," says Berry.

In his seven years with Berry, Joker was to acquire new skills and a growing reputation. First thing Berry did was to register the horse with the Appaloosa Horse Club. But he says they already had a "Joker" in the files, so he added his own initial, B for Berry, to make the Joker B. name complete. Basically, Joker B. was still a cowhorse but Berry "calf-roped on him at rodeos in Barstow, Victorville, Mojave, Red Mountain and Bishop. I used to loan him to a few Nevada cowboys (who knew him before I got him) to bulldog off at rodeos."

Because of his exceptional disposition, Berry and his wife also developed an unusual "act" involving Joker B. Berry began putting the horse into a pen with a large Brahman bull and the animals got to be fast friends. Wasn't long before they would appear in public with Mrs. Berry riding Joker and Berry riding the bull. This was an eye-opener in many a California parade and soon the Berrys began to get more requests for appearances than they could handle.

One such appearance was delayed by what Berry recalls as the most spectacular "wreck" Joker B. ever got into. It was

During the time Joker B. was owned by Lee Berry, he was primarily a cowhorse. However, as this photo indicates, Mr. and Mrs. Berry had spare-time fun riding the spotted stallion in parades, leading a Brahman bull. Berry rode the bull. They were frequently called upon to make public appearances.

early one morning when he was loading the already-saddled stud into a stock trailer, alongside the bull. Ordinarily they rode well side by side. But on this morning Joker got excited for some unknown reason and backed away—backed straight through the door to an underground storm cellar. Berry was horrified to see and hear his stud tumble head over heels, backward, down the steps into the deep cellar.

Hurrying into the cellar, Berry watched for the dust to settle—and there stood Joker, calmly surveying the wreckage, as though nothing had happened. "First I was patting on him and worried about him being hurt," Berry chuckles now. "Then when I saw he was alright I started cussing him."

Berry led the horse back up the steps. As they reached the top, a low-hanging beam snagged the saddle horn still in place on Joker's back. Tipping the stallion off balance, it caused him to tumble once again, backward, down into the storm cellar!

Beside himself with concern, Berry was astonished to find that Joker was still unhurt. This time he got the unsaddled horse loaded and off they went for a day at the rodeo, none the worse for the morning's gymnastics.

In view of such experiences as that—combined with Joker's range work in rough country cow-handling—it isn't surprising that Berry considered Joker B. tough as "whet leather." By 1953 he also had acquired something of a reputation as a sire, having fathered some spotted colts in the meantime.

Bill Benoist of Long Beach, California, had one such colt — and he wanted more. He thus became Joker B.'s seventh owner for a $1,500 purchase price, says Benoist, and began breeding the stallion at a $50 stud fee. The fee went to $100 the second year, then later to $250.

Fully mature, Joker B. had something of a dual personality, Benoist tells us. "Under a saddle, he was like a gelding. He was real mild, you could stack kids on him. They'd fall off and he'd just stand there. We could haul mares with him and have no problems. But at the breeding barn he was all business."

And during this period, Joker B. got a chance to again demonstrate his great speed. At the age of thirteen, Benoist matched him twice at Los Alamitos against young Quarter Horses and only got beat twice in eight races. At the national Appaloosa show in Quincy, California, Joker was entered in the 220—and won it despite pulling up a little sore.

Again, the horse—now roughly equivalent to a middle-aged man—was taken to the nationals at Deer Lodge, Montana, where he was entered in a four-horse race. All four finished in a knot that you could cover with a blanket, says Benoist. Joker B. was fourth, Apache won the race. So they matched Joker B. against Apache in the 220, Benoist recalls and "Joker won by plenty of daylight."

This was not, of course, the first clue to Joker B.'s quick speed. He had been accepted for registration in the American Quarter Racing Association November 4, 1949, during the time that Lee Berry owned him. His pedigree makes it clear that he was bred to sprint and his earlier rodeo contest work demonstrated his ability to catch a calf or a steer. Benoist also used Joker for team roping and he continued to enjoy a reputation as a good dogging horse.

By the late 1950s, Joker B. had also begun to acquire renown as a sire of both colorful and well-conformed Appaloosas. During the time Benoist owned him he sired the famed Jessie Joke, later a national champion mare; Joker Boy, the stout south Texas stallion; Mr. J. B., M. J. B., and Moka B. Some of the other California offspring of Joker B.'s that attracted national attention were Flying Star, Ardajoke, and Joker's Snow Patches, to name a few.

Had his career ended at this point, Joker B. would have been considered as a leading stallion of his time. But at a relatively advanced age, Joker B. changed hands again—and the stage was set for his rise to international prominence.

It happened at the San Antonio Stock Show in 1959. Carl Miles, an Abilene oil man, bought Joker B. for a reported $10,000 and moved the stallion to his Cee Bar Appaloosa Ranch near Celina, Texas. The stallion's duties included more than being a sire. Joker B. won more championships at halter before retiring from the show ring. He was ridden in parades by famous public officials, movie stars, opera queens. He appeared in motion pictures. He was the center of attention in a NBC telecast of the "Today Show." His fame rapidly snowballed as promotional opportunities arose and within a very few years after Miles bought him, Joker B. was in fact the best-known Appaloosa in the United States. Advertising and promotion cost money, of course, and if Joker B. hadn't helped pay his way, he could have been an expensive horse indeed. As it was, Miles' faith in the horse's investment potential was not misplaced. Joker certainly earned his keep.

By the end of June, 1964, according to Miles' reports, thirty-eight head of Joker B. colts had sold for a total of $201,675. This would be an apparent average of $5,307 per head. Since Miles did not get his first Joker B. colt crop until 1960, it is obvious that he didn't waste any time with his breeding program. In his first colt crop (of 1960) for Miles, Joker B. sired thirteen head. Two died at birth. Eight of the others became famed show winners in their own right. This group included Joker's Humdinger, Joker's Sundance, Joker's Sleepy, Joker Jack, Joker's Miss Reed, Joker's Cindy Cee, Joker's Star B and Joker's Alpha. Some of the stallions in this group have now turned out to be major sires of the Appaloosa breed themselves.

As his production proved his ability to transmit conformation, breeding and speed, Joker B. began to be visited by outside, high-quality mares in large numbers. They came from all over the United States and they came in all types. It is no wonder that within just a few years, you could hardly find an area of the United States where Joker B. offspring weren't

45

either showing at halter, competing in the arena contests, racing or being used to work cattle. Texas, of course, quickly came to be Joker B. country. In 1963, for example, the Top Ten competition of the Texas Appaloosa Horse Club found Joker B. colts commanding no less than *sixteen* of the divisions. That year also saw a Joker B. filly, Joker's Moneca, win ten out of fourteen starts on southwestern race tracks. She wound up setting three Appaloosa track records. From a conformation standpoint, four of the Top Ten halter Appaloosas in Texas in 1963 were sired by Joker B., including the high point horse and runner-up high point horse. The same was true of performance contests; Joker B. sired both the high point performance horse and the reserve winner. In 1965 Joker B. won the Premier Sire Award #1 created by the Texas Appaloosa Horse Club. And by this time Joker B. had become virtually an industry all by himself. He did not, of course, produce a champion by every single mare and some Joker B. colts didn't turn up with spots. But his batting average was so high and, in the case of all those champions, so spectacular that even his color failures had economic value—especially the mares who might later produce spotted colts with the right kind of cross.

Space prevents the listing of all the registered sons and daughters of Joker B. However, the writer obtained a list from the Appaloosa Horse Club of Moscow, Idaho, of all numbered Joker B. colts as of June 1, 1967, and that list included the names of 139 animals.

Having earned more honors and recognition than most any western horse in modern times, there were only a few pinnacles yet available to Joker B. One of these came November 20, 1965, when—for the only time in his life—the spotted stallion was sold at public auction and was syndicated.

It was the climax to Miles' fifth annual auction sale. He hated to sell the horse, Miles made clear, but his oil business

When public officials, movie stars and beauty queens needed a horse both eye-catching and easily-managed, they were delighted to climb on board Joker B. Not all who rode the horse in parades could ride as expertly as Texas Governor John Connally but in Joker's case it didn't matter. Child or adult could stay in the saddle and the big quiet stallion always brought his noted riders back in good shape

kept him gone so much of the time that he had to reduce his operation.

But Carl couldn't cut loose from Joker entirely—and when the sale ended, the horse had sold for $26,500 to a four-man syndicate, one of whom was Carl Miles. The other members were Frank Horlock, Jr. and John Lyle of Houston and Jack Ryan of Corpus Christi, Texas. They announced that Joker B.'s book was closed to outside mares.

In his final season at stud—1966—Joker B. continued to breed sound and settled more than a dozen of the syndicate's mares. Through much of the year he stayed in good health and a steady stream of people traveled long distances to see an animal that had become a legend in his own time.

Finally, at about 8 p.m. the night of July 13, 1966, death claimed the horse that had typified the Appaloosa to millions of Americans. It was reported that he died of a heart attack. He was buried at Cedar Hill Farms near Willis, Texas, and a monument was ordered for the grave site.

The impact of Joker B. on the Appaloosa breed is still to be fully evaluated. There is no question, however, but that it will be far-reaching and permanent. Decades from now, as a longer look at history brings our present into sharp focus, he is apt to be considered the leading moulder and shaper of the spotted horse in North America. Certainly, he dramatized and —through Miles' efforts—publicized the Appaloosa horse nationally as had never been done before. Praise about Joker B. during his lifetime sometimes became extravagant, as it often becomes about any champion. But in truth Joker B. did come mighty close to winning it all. ▲

6

KING P-234

Byrne James and his wife were driving down a street in Laredo, Texas, one day in the early 1930s when they saw a yearling colt they *had* to own. He was a blood bay colt with black mane and tail and black feet. Here was royalty on four legs.

A Mexican boy led the yearling down the dusty thoroughfare at a walk. James slowed his car for a better look. Yes, it *was* quite a colt. And they followed the boy and the colt all the way to their destination—the home of a Laredo horseman named Charlie Alexander. There, after a brief bargaining session, they bought the yearling for $300.

It turned out this was no run-of-the-mill cow pony. Alexander had acquired him from the Mamie Benevides Ranch at Laredo, and the youngster was a son of the noted running sire, Zantanon. That $300 James paid for the colt was a flock of currency in those days and no doubt some of his neighbors in the sagebrush and rattlesnake country around the James Ranch at Encinal might have figured Byrne got the short end of the deal.

Turned out this was more than just another horse. He was to become King P-234, the most famous Quarter Horse that ever lived.

Once back at the James Ranch, Byrne's missus didn't take long to hang a name on the yearling. "You've heard the expression 'King of Beasts'? Well, to me, he was the King — superior to all the rest..." Some thirty-five years later she recalled that the colt was a good-natured kind with an even disposition, "yet a good stallion."

In those days Byrne James was a professional baseball player in the spring and summer and a rancher the rest of the time. There was plenty of hard work to be done running cattle and in those days it was mostly still done on horseback. As soon as he was big enough, young King found himself with a saddle and a ranch hand on his back, doing general ranch work. King's future as a sire of "registered" Quarter Horses wasn't even dreamed of. The formation of the Quarter Horse registry was still some seven years in the future.

"In those days," James remembers, "ranchmen used horses for work. Very few of us ever took the trouble to find out the exact breeding on one."

But James did take the trouble to find out about King. Not only that but he took the trouble to go out and buy both the sire and the dam of that colt. He paid $500 for Zantanon and he also acquired Jabalina, (by The Strait Horse) King's dam. Further, James put a bunch of miles on his car to establish that the colt "... is bred just like his papers say he is bred." The colt's birthdate was June 2, 1931. Byrne was to own two full sisters of King before the young stallion passed into other hands. One of these came to a tragic end.

"She was about nine or ten months old," as James recalls, "and we had to rope her to get a hackamore on her. She fell over backward and broke her neck."

King's other full sister, Maria Elena, had a long and productive career as a broodmare, producing some outstanding colts.

What delighted Byrne James and other ranchmen in the area was that King represented an ideal stock horse, despite the fact that his sire was a small horse. Zantanon has been described as standing slightly under fourteen hands in height. Yet he was, in his prime, a heavy muscled animal of excellent balance and conformation. Many of his colts, including King, inherited his muscle and some had more height to boot. King's

This is the classic photo of King P-234, taken in his later years and the most widely-reproduced photo of King ever made. The stallion's quality is apparent and his conformation was to set the standard for Quarter Horse judging and breeding for more than a decade.

dam, Jabalina, stood fifteen hands or taller.

As King reached maturity, says James, he stood between 14.2 and fifteen hands and weighed from 1,150 to 1,200 pounds. By that time, King's obvious quality had attracted wide attention in the south Texas area.

King became a roping horse in 1933 partly because of James' pro baseball career. When he took off his boots in favor of baseball spikes that year he decided to loan King to a friend and neighbor, Win DuBose. In those days, DuBose was one of the good young ropers in that part of Texas — where roping has long been almost a way of life. And while Byrne James played infield for the New York Giants, his young stallion was back home learning to "rate" a calf. The work

In this early photo, Win DuBose rides the young King when he was being trained as a roping horse. Here they work on slow Jerseys— fast Brahmans came later. A neighbor of DuBose's, Lester Gilleland, was another south Texan who put training into the young stallion.

came easy to King. Win DuBose, who lives near Uvalde, Texas, remembers how easy it was to teach the horse.

"He was very quick to learn," remembers DuBose, "and good natured for a stallion. He had a lot of cow sense. I wouldn't say he was the fastest horse I ever rode but there was no lost motion. He was quick out of the box and quick to get to a calf.

"A neighbor named Lester Gilleland and I would take turns roping calves in the arena and after about thirty days we started taking him to small ropings... at first we had used a hackamore bit on him but then we changed to metal."

Soon Win and another roper, Johnny Stevens, were hauling King to the tough ropings throughout west and southwest Texas and they were winning their share. By the time Byrne James got home from the baseball wars he could see that friend DuBose wanted to own the stallion. And so King changed hands for the third time, on this occasion bringing $500.

"That was a big price then," James smiles now. "We were in the depths of the depression."

During the following eighteen months that Win DuBose owned King he recalls breeding about twenty-five mares to the stallion ". . . but we didn't keep a record, not knowing at the time that Quarter Horses would ever be registered.

"After a few years," DuBose wrote in 1966, "most of his (King's) colts in this immediate vicinity were bought and taken away. . . I sold every direct offspring of King's that I

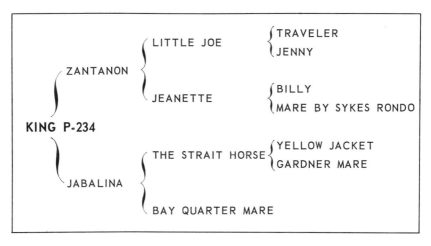

owned and started breeding a few mares to King April, owned by Morris Witt."

While he owned King, DuBose stood him to outside mares at a stud fee of $10. And sometimes, unusual as it may seem today, he would keep visiting mares as long as three months —free.

One of the things about King that intrigued DuBose in the summer was the horse's color. Gold flecks would show up in King's bay coat, giving him a striking sheen. "I never saw another like that," he says.

In 1937, when there was still no hint of the booming Quarter Horse industry two decades in the future, Win DuBose decided to sell King. He had been in conversation with Jess Hankins of Rocksprings, Texas, a few times about that subject but DuBose understandably was not eager to let a producing stallion go. Still, money was always needed and a man couldn't own them *all.*

In July Win told Jess he would sell the horse. The agreed-upon price was $800. The deal hit Hankins at precisely the worst time.

"I had just that day spent all the money I had for a bunch of calves," Hankins recalled later. "So I borrowed the money from Lowell . . ." (Lowell Hankins, Jess' brother). The deal was closed July 7, 1937.

Not just everybody figured in 1937 that a cowhorse was worth any $800. "People said I was crazy and would go broke," Jess chuckled long afterward. For a few years there, of course, King did not create any surge of wealth for the Hankins family. The stallion was offered at a $15 stud fee the first year of breeding. Jess raised the fee to $25 the next year—although he remembers "I didn't get too many mares in those days at *any* price."

But the south Texan hadn't bought the horse on a whim. "I liked his conformation," Hankins says, "and I hadn't seen a horse around like him. I saw his colts — he was producing some fine ones by all kinds of mares — and he had the speed to produce fast horses too."

King is shown at right and the mare on the left is Maria Elena, his full sister. She later became an outstanding broodmare for Jess Hankins. King had one other full sister. She died in an accident while still a filly.

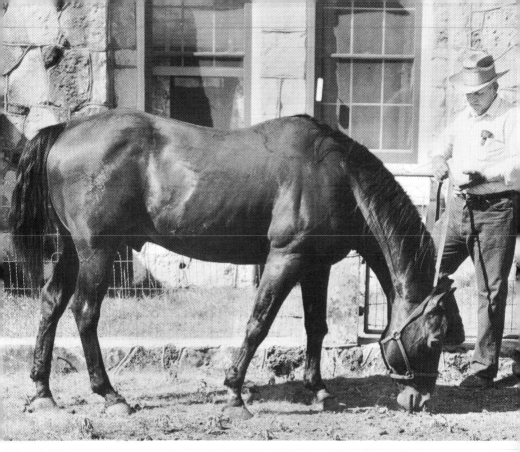

In the 1940s and 1950s, the name of King and the Jess Hankins breeding operation became synonymous. Noted for a calm, settled disposition, King became very much a part of the Hankins family.

As the years passed and the Quarter Horse registry was formed (in 1940) King began to produce the colts that would make him the most famous sire of the breed. It would take pages to list them all. At the time of his death, King had produced 520 registered foals.

In Jess Hankins' own judgement, two horses that helped establish King's breeding fame were his sons Poco Bueno and Royal King—both great sires in their own right. By the fine mare Queen H, King produced Squaw H and Hank H, outstanding running horses. And 89er by King also ran and produced running horses.

But it was in the conformation and "doing" department this stallion joined the ranks of the immortal breeding animals. Consider these other King colts, picked at random: Old

Taylor, Captain Jess, Little Tom B., King Joe Boy, Beaver Creek, Major King and Zantanon H. Among his outstanding broodmares was O'Quinn's Midget, one of the few Quarter mares ever to produce *six* AAA offspring.

At his death, King had sired Quarter Horses which thoroughly dominated most phases of the breed's performance activity—particularly cutting competition. Among his get were forty-six Register of Merit qualifiers, eleven of which earned their AQHA Championships. On the list of leading sires of cutting horses, from 1951 to 1956, King led with twenty-four qualifiers. Poco Bueno by King was second with twenty-four and Royal King by King was third with sixteen. Another of his sons, Kings Joe Boy, was fifth with seven qualifiers.

Statistics, however, fail to fully measure this animal's impact on the Quarter Horse breed. Space prohibits a full list, not only of his own get, but of the thousands of third and fourth generations of King-bred horses that are today the living proof of his potency and quality. Further, the animal's appearance and the performance of his offspring excited the imagination of thousands of new horse owners in the 1950s when the breed began to grow rapidly—and the term "King-bred" became a household phrase among horsemen.

Near the end of his long career, owner Jess Hankins could legitimately advertise King P-234 as the "Cornerstone of an Industry." That many shared this view was proved by the number of owners who paid substantial fees in the 1950s to get a colt by King. His breeding fee at the time of his death was $2,500.

To the Hankins family, the stallion represented a lot more than a successful investment. He was one *of* the family. He remained a gentle horse all of his life and Jess often noted that "any kid who had ever handled a horse could ride him." Mrs. Hankins remembers too that there was one thing in particular King liked: "Every time Jess went out to the corral, he'd stick his head over Jess' shoulder — for his ears to be cleaned out."

At the age of twenty-six, King's life ended—March 24, 1958. He died of a heart attack. Noted the *Quarter Horse Journal:* "No other stallion now living can boast such a record as King's and only time will tell when another will equal it."▲

7

LEO

Those who knew him best remember John Tillman of Pawhuska, Oklahoma, as a gentleman of the old school. When he practiced criminal law, he was a hard-driving, tightly-wound man of intense concentration. Like many successful and prominent people, he had one overriding, spare-time passion.

It was horse racing.

Nothing was more of a vacation to Tillman than spending his spare hours, usually Sunday afternoons, at the Pawhuska Fairgrounds. The straightaway race track there, at the bottom of a grassy slope, was ideal for match races up to 300 yards. And in the early 1940s, this track was the scene of most of the famous Oklahoma match races of this century.

If John (who died in 1964) could have selected a period in his life when he enjoyed racing the most, he might well have picked the years 1942 and 1943. He had bought himself a two-year-old sorrel colt in south Texas, name of Leo. The colt had started winning every race he ran, from 220 up to 300 yards.

Within months, the word went out that the horse to beat in Oklahoma was this Leo colt. Soon, John Tillman let it be known that Leo was "open to the world" at any distance up to 300 yards. Racehorse men from all over the southwest got the word. Many decided they had a colt good enough to "run at" Leo.

"Just bring your horse and your money," smiled Tillman. And nearly all those who did went home less prosperous. It wasn't that Tillman wanted their money. A generous man, he was like many racing enthusiasts: He loved the sport for its own sake. He loved to win.

Living in Pawhuska was another racing fan named Bill Row, who shared both Tillman's friendship and his passion for winning a "short" race. Row does not remember when it was he decided that there just *had* to be a horse that could beat Leo. But somewhere, he knew, there was. Or maybe more. Soon Row and Max Michaelis of Kyle, Texas, were looking for horses to give Leo some competition. They looked, logically, in Louisiana. The Cajun country produced then, as now, more fine, quick little racehorses per square foot than anyplace on earth. Excepting maybe Oklahoma.

In those days, a steady stream of good running horses was coming out of Louisiana sired by Flying Bob and Doc Horn. So it was that on a fine Sunday in 1943, several thousand people gathered at the Pawhuska track to see Leo take on the latest comer.

Tillman knew good horse flesh when he saw it. And as he watched jockey Claude Hart mount a little blood bay mare named Punkin, John knew Leo had himself a race. His stud was being ridden by the able Walter Dentist, Leo's jockey in many of his victories. Bill Row and Michaelis covered John's $1,000 bet and also those of many Pawhuska folks, who had found Leo a most profitable weekend investment.

The race was for 220 yards as jockey Hart remembers it. And Punkin stumbled coming out of the gates. But she recovered quickly, made up the ground in driving strides and whipped by Leo to win by half a length. This was Leo's first loss in more than a dozen wins and there was very little rejoicing that night in Pawhuska.

But hope springs eternal in the racing fraternity and during the week that followed, a sizeable body of opinion developed that any horse can have an off day, including Leo. True, Punkin was by the noted Flying Bob. Now, this new mare that Row and Michaelis were going to run at Leo. . .well, it might be a different story.

Might have been, but wasn't. Came another Sunday afternoon, again Walter Dentist was up on Leo. This time the race

The Orren Mixer painting of Leo shows him against a background of fine broodmares and offspring. In his first breeding season, as a matter of fact, Leo was turned out for pasture breeding to ranch mares. Daughters of Leo quickly established their supremacy as broodmares when their offspring developed into both racing and working Quarter Horses.

was for 300 yards. Again, Claude Hart rode the challenging mare. Again, several thousand turned out for the match. They called this mare Lady. Like Punkin, she was about 14.3. A daughter of Doc Horn, slimmer than Punkin, she weighed perhaps 1,000 pounds. Leo, at full maturity, stood about 14.2 and weighed about 1,100 pounds. He was a stout, good-backed young horse in 1943 and could carry a 130 pound jockey like the wind.

Squatting along the fence, Pawhuska's sportsmen put their money up. Again Tillman's faith in Leo was worth $1,000, and once more Bill and Max covered the bets against their mare.

59

Representative of Leo's ability to sire both speed and quality are
Croton Oil (above) and Connie Leo. Croton Oil in 1966 was the
leading Leo sire of Racing Register of Merit offspring. Among her
running and working produce, Connie Leo foaled a stud colt and a
filly that turned out to be both AAA racehorses and AQHA Champions. She was a AAA running mare herself. Croton Oil's dam,
Randle's Lady, was one of the only horses ever to beat Leo in a
match race.

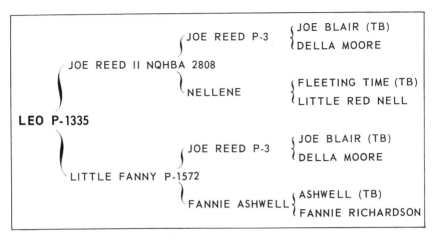

The two horses broke clean from the gate and ran shoulder to shoulder in a sprint that took perhaps sixteen seconds. At the finish line, Claude Hart remembers, Lady had Leo beat soundly.

There would be another meeting between Leo and Lady in future years, with far different results. For the moment, it had been proved that Leo was not invincible. But if anything, these defeats may have improved the stallion's earning capacity.

Records are lacking to prove it but other and slower horses ran at Leo after these two encounters and were left in the dust. Within a few months, as a matter of fact, John Tillman had to face an incredible fact: He could not find any more takers for match races. Leo had won twenty out of twenty-two races. Lacking any kind of pari-mutuel tracks to run on, Leo had virtually run himself out of a job.

"We realized there would be a time when Leo would be a great stud," said Tillman's daughter years later. "But we had no place in the country to keep a horse then."

When Tillman sold the horse to Enrique Salinas of Eagle Pass, Texas, for a reported $2,000, some Oklahoma horsemen may have guessed that this was all anybody would ever hear of the promising young stallion. If so, it was the worst guess of the century. You can hardly find a major Quarter Horse breeder today in the United States who doesn't own some Leo-bred mares. Possibly no other stallion of the breed is so widely respected for producing good broodmares as the stud whose only significant track defeats were at the hands of two mares.

Leo was no fluke. His speed and quality measured up to his pedigree. He began life in company with other good-bred horses at the J. W. House breeding farm at Cameron, Texas, birthplace of many horses destined for greatness in the southwest. Leo's sire was Joe Reed II, a son of the noted Joe Reed P-3. Mother of Joe Reed II was Nellene, by the Thoroughbred stud, Fleeting Time. Photos of Joe Reed II show the kind of horse that can sprint at the track—or put a calf roper to the pay window. His colts did both.

Leo's mother was equally well-regarded by the old time horsemen. She was Little Fanny, a daughter also of Joe Reed P-3, and her dam also was by a Thoroughbred. Little Fanny was quite a mother, producing rodeo horses, running horses and prolific stallions. Besides Leo, she produced a full sister named Little Sister W, the running horses Bill Reed and Ashwood. Other Little Fanny colts were Tick Tack, Tucson and Sassy Time.

By the time he was eighteen months old, Leo was running at Eagle Pass, Texas, owned by Lester J. Manning of Gatesville. Manning bought the colt at sixteen months of age from Colonel House for $325. "...I spotted the colt in a stall at House's place," he remembered years later, "and I fell for him."

Leo's first race at Eagle Pass saw him running away from the pack at 220 yards. Against a field of eight colts, said Manning, Leo covered the distance in 12.7 seconds, easily daylighting the place horse. "He was the most perfect gate horse I ever saw in my life," Manning told the writer in 1967. "And he could do things I never saw another horse do...like he could pop his hind foot up against his stomach to hit flies."

It was at Eagle Pass that Oklahoma trainer Bill Morgan saw the colt and reported his merits to John Tillman in Pawhuska. Tillman authorized a purchase price of $675 and Leo started for Oklahoma.

It was coincidental that after Tillman's successful match racing of Leo, the horse would be sold right back to Eagle

Except for his bad knee, Leo in his final years continued in good flesh and showed the conformation that helped make his get contenders for halter honors.

Pass. But that is what happened. A banker, Enrique Salinas, apparently bought the stallion for racing purposes primarily—and the year was probably 1944. There is at least a record noting that Leo ran at the Eagle Pass track in 1944, doing 300 yards in :16.5.

Leo was to change owners three more times before he found a permanent home. His ultimate owner, Bud Warren, recalls seeing the young stud at Eagle Pass—and it did not seem to Warren that the animal was getting proper care. This was noticed too by other alert horsemen and not many months passed before Bill Row himself negotiated to buy Leo. It cost him $2,000, Row remembered later, but he was glad to get the horse back to Pawhuska. Starting about 1943, Leo had been bred to several mares and by 1946 Leo colts had started arriving at the tracks. One of his early colts was the great producing broodmare, Flit, now considered famous for her champion offspring by different stallions.

Initially, Leo was used in simple herd improvement. In his first breeding season the horse was loaned to August W. Lohmann of Foraker, Oklahoma, who pasture-bred his ranch mares to the stud. Later, Row's ranching operation included New Mexico properties—and Leo went farther west. Not for long. Again, from Oklahoma, came a Leo fan—Gene Moore. "Gene came down to Carlsbad and talked me out of Leo and gave me $2,000," chuckled Row, twenty years later. This time the stud went to Fairfax, Oklahoma. Somewhere along the line Leo had acquired an injury to his right knee and by 1947 his racing days were over. Now he was either a breeding horse or nothing.

Bud Warren remembers that he was interested in the horse but wasn't interested $2,500 worth. That was Moore's asking price. Several times Bud went to Moore's place to see the stud. Warren had never seen or met Gene Moore himself.

Finally, he drove by Gene's place in a pickup truck, determined to go ahead and buy the horse. Mrs. Moore said her husband was off up in Kansas buying cattle. By telephone, they located him—and in a few minutes the $2,500 selling price was agreed upon. Warren said that he had a pickup truck with him—or would Moore rather return and deliver the horse?

"Oh, you can go ahead and take him now," said Moore.

"Well," replied Warren, "who should I pay for him?"

"That's alright. I'll stop by your place in the next two or three weeks and get the money."

In this informal fashion Leo went to the Warren Ranch at Perry, Oklahoma, where he was to spend the next and final twenty years of his life. Several months later, Moore phoned Warren and said he could mail him a check for the horse, which Warren did. Moore was killed in an auto accident months later and Bud Warren never personally met the man from whom he purchased Leo.

If his stallion had been famous as a match racehorse, Leo was now to totally eclipse that fame by his record at stud. Within a decade or so, Leo offspring not only had excelled at the track—but more important from a breeding standpoint—his daughters had produced winners of all kinds. Some of the mares that came to him later were famous in their own right. Leo helped put others on the breeding map. Significantly, though, very few of the early mares he was bred to were outstanding running mares. Said Warren in 1962:

"Up to four or five years ago, to our knowledge, Leo had not been bred to a mare that had seen a race track. At that time he was leading the Register of Merit sire list with about one hundred.

"We just haven't gotten top mares, stakes mares. And we still aren't. We have bred a few of the good mares through the years. Bright Eyes was bred to Leo once, Stella Moore once, Barbara L, Miss Wonder Bar..."

By the twilight of his career, however, some of the nation's finest Quarter mares had been bred to Leo—and they and their offspring produced halter and performance horses as well as racehorses. For example, Leo's daughter Flit mothered the first World Champion Cutting Horse Stallion, King's Pistol. One of Leo's sons, named Leob, was considered to have the kind of cow sense that you usually find in a Jessie James or Hollywood Gold.

Leo helped add speed to other stock horse bloodlines. The fine mare 89er by King P-234 had seven of her eleven ROM racing offspring by Leo. Another King mare, Betty Warren, had four ROM foals by Leo and another by his son, Leo Tag. Three of Sorrel Sue's ROM produce were by Leo and the other two by Leo Tag. She was a King mare too and the dam of the AQHA champion, Okie Leo.

Some of the great mares that went to Leo had spectacular production records at his court. Yeager's Lady JA produced three of her five AAA-rated offspring by Leo. Swamp Angel by Grano de Oro had four ROMs by Leo. O'Quinn's Midget, who produced champions by nearly every major Quarter Horse stallion, had two AAA-rated mares by Leo. One, Leo's Midget, produced one of the hottest two-year-olds of 1962, Miss Bar Leo, who ran at Denver in world record time.

Leo-bred horses really caused the Quarter Horse world to look twice as they collected world championships. Miss Meyers by Leo was World Champion Quarter Running Mare. Palleo Pete by Leo won the World Champion title for Quarter running stallions. Dari Star and Dari Man, both from Leo mares, won the racing world championship for geldings. Another Leo mare produced three world champions by herself—Vanetta Dee, Vanna Bar and Vandy's Flash. Vanetta Dee won three world championships for racing.

Yet, interestingly enough, it is probably true that Leo never did get in his entire life as many race mares as, say, Three Bars might have had in his book in just one season. It happened repeatedly that mares of ordinary pedigree would produce, by Leo, both running horses and those that developed later into fine broodmares. Quarter Horse association records testify to his place in the breed.

For the period 1949 through 1966, Leo was the leader

among maternal grandsires of Register of Merit qualifiers in racing. No less than 122 of his daughters produced ROM qualifiers and those daughters had produced a whopping 257 qualifiers.

He also was second leading sire in ROM racing qualifiers. Two hundred and three Leo get were ROM and among that group some seventy-eight were AAA-rated. Only Top Deck and Three Bars, both registered Thoroughbreds attracting running-type mares, sired more AAA colts than Leo. Yet today Leo is known almost as widely for his halter and "doing horses" as for producing running ability. For example, Leo is second among maternal grandsires of AQHA Champions. He had twenty-three, through 1966. Only King P-234, with thirty-five, ranked higher.

What's more, Leo himself ranked fourth among sires of AQHA Champions and was tied for third among leading sires of 1966 ROM performance qualifiers.

By the 1960s, these statistics had helped make Leo blood a good buy and his colts from proven producers were bringing $10,000 or more at the Warren ranch. His stud fee had gone to $2,500. Leo colts were running at race tracks, were being used for roping in top rodeo competition, in cutting, in all other phases of Quarter Horse performance contests.

He was in the view of many the most important living sire of the Quarter Horse breed. Then on May 13, 1967, Bud Warren reported that his age and infirmities required that Leo had to be put to sleep.

When he knew the end for Leo was coming, Warren recalled an old broodmare he had owned for some years. She was an important part of the Leo story. Now twenty-nine years of age and living out her life on good pasture, she grazed not far from Leo's stall. By Leo, this old mare had produced the good stud, Croton Oil. Leo also had sired her fine daughters, South Pacific and Rosa Leo. The latter was AAA. Both mares later produced four AAA foals apiece.

Some may have known this old mare as Randle's Lady, her registered name. Others would have remembered her as Little Breeze. But there was the time when they called her Lady— and she was one of those two mares who back in 1943 at the Pawhuska fairgrounds demonstrated that even a great champion like Leo could come in second.▲

8

OKLAHOMA
STAR

May Day, 1916, may have been a dark day for millions of people concerned with the terrible war in Europe. But it was a glad day near Laverne, Oklahoma, on the homestead of Tommie Moore. His running mare, Cut Throat, had produced her foal and it was a dandy.

The little bay colt arrived wearing a star on his forehead. So Moore promptly dubbed him Oklahoma Star. This colt *should* have been a good one since he had a couple of distinguished parents. His sire was the Thoroughbred Dennis Reed, who was by Lobus by an imported running horse, Golden Garter. Sire of Golden Garter was the noted Ben d'Or. But what got the Oklahoma short-running boys interested in Dennis Reed was his early speed. Here was a miler who could run his first 440 yards in twenty-three seconds. It remained to be seen how much of that sprint the new arrival inherited from his daddy.

Everybody figured too that he ought to get plenty from his mother. Cut Throat had just about run herself out of competitors in Oklahoma and surrounding states. Laverne is not too far from parts of Texas, Kansas and Colorado, so Cut Throat's early history was one of running and winning at matched races and county fairs. To "graduate" to bigger purses, she needed a Thoroughbred number—and so eventually she became May

Matteson, somehow acquired a number, and became one of the most successful racing mares of her day.

In fact, one Quarter Horse researcher, Nelson Nye, reported that conservative bankers of the day would lend you money on her races since she was not considered a speculative investment. While some — who know bankers — may doubt that, what is unquestioned is that Cut Throat's speed at the short sprints would put her in the forefront of any graded race today. She covered 220 yards in eleven seconds and the quarter in twenty-two flat from a scoreline. Her name came from the wire cut that ripped across her windpipe while still a filly.

This mare was bred to run. She was by Gulliver by Missouri Rondo. Her dam was Money Spinner by the great Dan Tucker. So it was that Tommie Moore and family were *expecting* a champion that May morning in 1916. And they were not to be disappointed.

Oklahoma Star was a leggy colt on arrival but he did not reach any great height as he matured. Writer Bob Denhardt thought the horse somewhat larger than the 14.2 most people have recorded for Oklahoma Star and that he probably weighed under the 1,200 pounds that early observers have mentioned. Denhardt judged him to be under 1,100 pounds as a mature horse and thought that his Thoroughbred breeding was noticeable in his ears, head, withers and long bottom line. His quarter breeding was apparent in his heavily-muscled hindquarters, his pasterns and sloping rump. The stern muscle particularly would account for his blinding speed out of the chute.

However, the reader is given to understand that Oklahoma Star was not a halter champion in the sense that we know one today. Well-made and built for speed, he matched perfectly the mold of the period when he lived — a period when racing was not an industry at all in the southwest, particularly insofar as "short running" horses were concerned. Yet this colt was to become one of the truly prepotent sires of the Quarter Horse breed and produce offspring of consistent beauty as well as ability.

Star ran his first race as a two-year-old. Owner Moore expected plenty from the young stallion since his early-morning workouts proved his speed. And so Moore figured he might as

Oklahoma Star is pictured with his mother, the famed running mare, Cut Throat. Behind the colt is breeder Tommy Moore. The man at the halter is unknown.

well test the colt but good. He matched him against a proven racehorse named Slip Shoulder at 220 yards and Moore had no trouble getting all of his bets covered in a hurry. No one gave the untried colt much chance. And that is what makes ball games and elections and horse races. Slip Shoulder's backers couldn't figure out how come the newcomer wound up at that finish line first. And to make sure the race wasn't an accident they imported a mare from another county, named Kate Bernard and matched Oklahoma Star again, also at one-eighth of a mile.

Quarter Horse Historian Ed Bateman reported that Tommie Moore rode Star himself. It was common practice at the time for opponents to try and "buy" your jockey, so Moore was taking no chance—although he must have been pushing fifty at the time and weighed about 150 pounds. Nevertheless, the young

Oklahoma Star, shown here as a mature stallion, was a prolific producer but many of his get were not registered. As with many of the pre-Quarter Horse registry breeding animals, Oklahoma Star was used for upgrading ranch mares and records were poorly kept in some cases.

stallion came through, winning the 220 against the good mare in eleven seconds flat. Word about this dual win got around in a hurry and it caused the stallion's reputation to grow several notches. Wrote Bateman: "...the result was such that all the cowmen of that section concluded immediately Oklahoma Star was a better risk than big steers on cake and grass."

For more than a decade after that Oklahoma Star was active on the tracks of the southwestern states. More often than not his owner would ride him, despite his weight and years, and Star won most of his races. He beat such famous short-running

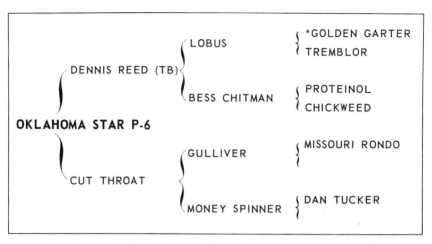

horses as Jimmy Hicks, Duck Hunter (by Peter McCue), Henry Star, Ned S and a host of others.

It was in 1925 that Moore sold the stallion for the substantial price of $500. However, the following year Moore got him back in a trade. And the horse had become, by then, an established sire. His offspring were making their own reputations and, equally important, the great champion cowboys of the day were seeking Oklahoma Star blood for their contest horses. Rodeo men like Bob Crosby, Ike Rude, Dick Truitt, Jess Goodspeed and Clyde Burke were using Star-bred horses.

Like so many of the immortals in the horse world, Star has had his greatness confirmed through his descendants. Significantly, he produced all types of working and running horses as well as future halter champions. Star Deck is an example of the beauty he stamped on his get and is another indication how some of the foundation sires, although not of perfect conformation themselves, could sire conformation horses.

Oklahoma Star changed hands once more during his lifetime. He was sold to Ronald Mason in 1926 and lived to the ripe old age of twenty-seven. He died in 1943. When the American Quarter Horse Association was formed in 1940, it was decided that the first nineteen numbers in the stud book should be set aside for the widely-recognized foundation sires then alive. Oklahoma Star was assigned the sixth spot on the roster, hence his P-6 number.

In assessing this horse's contribution to Quarter Horsedom

it is unfortunate that not all his offspring could be properly identified. Since the AQHA registry was not formed until near the end of his life, many great descendants will never be known for sure. One unregistered example was the nationally-famous Old Baldy horse, by Oklahoma Star, Jr. However, the list of Oklahoma Star get that is known makes a roll call of royalty.

Writing in *The Quarter Horse Journal* in 1963, Bob Denhardt recorded the fact that Oklahoma Star had few peers as a breeding horse. Some seventy-nine of his get were registered. Among them were such horses as the following, with the number of each one's registered get:

Sizzler — P-160	— 88 get
Oklahoma Star, Jr. — P-590	— 130
Starway — P-508	— 153
Osage Star — P-704	— 107
Star Deck — P-1343	— 193
Nowata Star — P-1606	— 312

Through these stallions as well as through his female offspring, Oklahoma Star helped produce dozens of ROM running horses, AQHA Champions, and the doing horses that today swell the arenas of Quarter Horse shows throughout the nation.▲

9

OLD SORREL

Bob Kleberg, Jr. smiled as he looked at the jumping course his King Ranch workmen had just erected.

It was an attractive circular affair with jumps at intervals, allowing the jump bars to go up to five feet.

It was really his wife's idea and the charming mistress of the huge south Texas spread was proud of it. Mrs. Kleberg had told her husband she wanted to breed some Thoroughbreds, just for jumping. Soon she had her jumping course and was busy planning to produce champions.

But, the story goes, Bob couldn't resist teasing his Mrs. a little bit.

"I have an old sorrel horse that should jump those things pretty well," he told her one day. Mrs. K. was understandably skeptical. So, forthwith, Kleberg ordered a fourteen year old stallion brought from the stables. The handler started to put on a jumping rig.

"Never mind that," Kleberg laughed. He flipped the halter rope over the stallion's neck, tied it on the other side and jumped up on the horse, bareback. He loped the stud with only a halter toward the jumps. Up and over he went, around the course, clearing the four-foot high bars with ease. It was the first—and doubtless the last—time that this horse ever ran a jumping course.

"How did you know he would jump?" asked Mrs. Kleberg, visibly impressed.

"Well," explained the King Ranch boss, "he'll sure jump prickly pear and mesquite. No reason why he wouldn't jump these."

This story has been told many times in the Kleberg family since the event took place some forty years ago. And it tells a lot about the most famous Quarter Horse ever owned by America's most famous ranch. Old Sorrel was the stallion's name—the foundation sire of the entire King Ranch breeding program of Quarter Horses.

But he was a cowhorse before anybody knew him as a sire. He knew the feel of brush country sand under his feet. He stayed a stallion instead of becoming a gelding because he proved himself first as the kind of horse any cowboy would love to throw his saddle on. That's how they judged a working horse in cow country half a century ago—and it is how they still judge one on the King Ranch.

A young veterinarian arrived at the ranch at about the same time Old Sorrel got there. His name was J. K. Northway and today, more than half a century later, Doctor Northway is still there. He remembers the sorrel colt well and how he became a legend.

It was in 1916 that young Robert J. Kleberg, Jr., convinced his cousin Caesar that a certain colt owned by George Clegg of Alice, Texas, would make a top cowpony. The colt was a beauty, no question about that. He had some size to him, refinement, action. He was alert. His disposition was clearly excellent.

The colt came by his quality honestly. Hickory Bill, his sire, and one of the greatest sons of Peter McCue, put some leg under the colt. He would certainly have speed. Old Sorrel's dam was a Dr. Rose mare owned by Clegg. Not much is known about her ancestry except that she came from Kentucky and probably had some Thoroughbred ancestors.

So the deal was made and the Klebergs paid George Clegg $125 for the sorrel colt. It was seventy-five miles from Clegg's ranch near Alice, Texas, to the King Ranch spread and there were no trucks available in those days. Nor trains nor much of any other kind of transportation—except feet. And that's how the sorrel colt came to the ranch. He was led all seventy-

Working cowhorses were, and still are, vitally important to major cattle operations like the giant King Ranch. Robert J. (Bob) Kleberg, Jr., rides an Old Sorrel descendant in above photo, doing the kind of job the Quarter Horse was bred to do. All King Ranch horses are heavy in the blood of Old Sorrel.

five miles, following his momma, to his new home. Nobody recalls the trip bothering mare or colt.

As he grew and developed, Bob Kleberg and King Ranch hands recognized in the colt more than just another mount for a day's work. He grew strong and tough on hard work and hard play.

"I saw them rope off him and ride him all morning," recalls Doctor Northway, "then race him in the afternoon." Old Sorrel spent the first couple of years of his life growing up in the remuda of working horses. His future as a sire was even then apparent. Everybody wanted to ride him, because he was a cowboy's kind of horse.

To understand how excited the Klebergs were to get a horse of this quality, disposition and stamina, it's necessary to dig into a little history. Most of it is well-known in Texas.

The good cowhorse was as vital to a cattle ranch in the 19th century as our cars are to us today. You couldn't work a thousand head of half-wild mother cows and calves out of brush country or dry creek beds without a tough mount under you.

These stallions, Babe Grande (above) and Macanudo, were sons of Old Sorrel and were used intensively to concentrate the sire's blood. Macanudo was out of a Hickory Bill daughter. Macanudo was mated mostly to mares by his half-brothers and out of Quarter Horse outcross mares. Most of the mares he was bred to were daughters of Cardinal, Little Richard and Solis. Babe Grande's dam was a Hickory Bill daughter. He was outbred to mares of Quarter Horse and Thoroughbred breeding and inbred to daughters and double granddaughters of Old Sorrel. His breeding raised the percentage of Old Sorrel genes in his colts to thirty-six per cent.

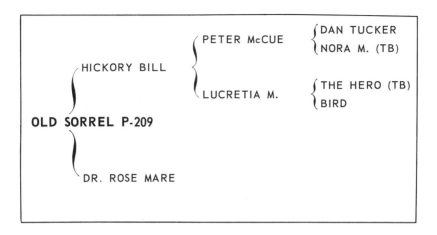

Multiply the average ranch by a hundred and you have the King Ranch of the old west. It covered more than a million acres at one time. It still measures 823,000 acres. But then the horse was as important as the cowboys who straddled them—and every rancher who drew breath stayed awake nights trying to figure out how to produce a horse to take the measure of the huge country, the incredible hours, the drouths, lack of good feed and hard-working cowboys.

Captain Richard King, immediately after the Civil War, began buying blooded stock from Kentucky to use on his vast Texas holdings. In 1868 he bought "blood-stallions to improve my horse stock... I paid as high as from three hundred to one thousand dollars."

The riverboat captain-turned-rancher did well with his early breeding effort. He picked the best little Spanish mustang mares he could find to mate with the long-legged Kentucky horses. He even separated them in at least one pasture as to color. He managed to boost the size of the offspring up to around fifteen hands from the fourteen-and-under mustang stock.

Such horses got popular in a hurry—and King had trouble holding on to them. He sold some and others disappeared. Captain King later testified that some 978 horses were stolen from his ranch in the three years from 1869 to 1872. Little wonder that early-day ranch owners all over the west became hard men. They used the hangman's noose on thousands of horse thieves throughout the west, and to call a man "horse thief" was to invite a fight, well into the 20th century.

After Captain King's death, his effort to find the ideal ranch horse continued under his descendants. The Klebergs and Sam Ragland are said to have tried nearly every breed of horse, in an effort to get the perfect specimen. Mostly, the ranch used Thoroughbred or Standardbred horses. Some Morgans and Arabians and saddle-bred animals were brought in too. In describing how the crosses fared, A. O. Rhoad and R. J. Kleberg, Jr. wrote in the *Journal of Heredity* in 1946:

"Thoroughbreds were widely utilized in grading-up. The first and second crosses on the Spanish mares developed by Captain King were especially good cow ponies. Many of the larger ones were valuable as light horses for driving. Although they did not have quite as much speed for short distances as the Standardbred, their endurance was great in the hot climate ... In spite of all the selection by two generations of good livestock managers, the crossbreeding program of crossing Standardbred and Thoroughbred horses on the good Spanish mares ... did not, on the average, improve the horses as cow horses. The contrary was true. Many were too big and leggy for ranch work, although they were still in demand by the army remount service and as carriage horses ... "

It wasn't that the programs were total failures. It was simply a matter of finding the precise combination of qualities the cowhorse needs. Perhaps we should call horses like Peter McCue, Steel Dust, Traveler, and Old Sorrel "genetic accidents." Certainly all the early Quarter Horse foundation sires were basically of Thoroughbred breeding—but it was not their speed that gave them fame. It was the magic they made through their offspring.

And so it was no wonder that Bob Kleberg rejoiced as it became clear that after more than half a century, the King Ranch had uncovered the single animal it would take to found a dynasty of ranch horses. Old Sorrel was that horse.

His first few colts, as he reached breeding age, seemed to confirm this. One was Celestino (or "Tino" for short) and the other Melon. They were by bred-up ranch mares and they showed exceptional quality.

But Bob Kleberg had seen other stallions that crossed well too, yet the blood went flat after the first generation. Old Sorrel would have to prove he was no one-cross wonder. To be certain that he got a complete test, the stallion was bred to fifty of the best handling and doing mares on the King Ranch. Mostly, these were mares of Thoroughbred or part-Thoroughbred breeding. The results were good—and at this point began one of the fascinating, often controversial developments in the King Ranch program: inbreeding.

Some breeders look askance at the practice even today. But the Old Sorrel line jumped directly from *carefully-supervised* inbreeding and linebreeding. It's important that the qualification be kept in mind. The ranch aim was to concentrate and preserve the blood of Old Sorrel.

"The first important effort," wrote Rhoad and Kleberg later, "was made when Solis, one of Old Sorrel's sons out of a Thoroughbred mare was mated to his daughters from this same band of mares. In the course of a very short time, this band of mares was built up to thirty-five or forty in number and in this way Solis was mated to forty of his half-sisters mostly from Thoroughbred mares. The results of this mating were very gratifying and it was clear that a long stride toward a fixed type had been made in this first mating."

The possibility of genetic failure was not overlooked.

"They were fully aware that not every exceptional sire has a balance of genetic qualities which will stand the test of close inbreeding without disaster. The only way in which this could be determined was by actual trial. He (Old Sorrel) was mated on a few occasions to his best daughters and the results, while encouraging, were not exceptional.

"But when his son Solis was mated on Old Sorrel's daughters the results were so good that the management decided to try to perpetuate Old Sorrel through linebreeding and inbreeding."

So, on a large scale, the owners of Old Sorrel began and continued the breeding program that extends to this day. It is the oldest, continuous program of ranch horse production in

Peppy (above) and Wimpy P-1 were second generation King Ranch sires that were used to continue the ranch's large linebreeding and inbreeding program. Peppy was a grandson (through Little Richard) of Old Sorrel and a great grandson of the old horse through Cardinal. Peppy was bred primarily to daughters and double granddaughters of Old Sorrel. Wimpy had the honor of being awarded P-1, first registration number of the American Quarter Horse Association in 1941. Wimpy's foals out of Old Sorrel daughters are 62.5 per cent related to him.

If any photos of Old Sorrel in his prime were taken they have yet to turn up. This is the only picture available of the horse and was taken, obviously, in his last years. He was still breeding, though, and sired Hired Hand at the age of thirty.

the Quarter Horse world. And some of the stars in that program turned into exceptional stallions in their own right — horses like Solis, Cardinal, Little Richard, Macanudo, Babe Grande, and Hired Hand. In the second generation, names like Peppy and Wimpy P-1 (Wimpy received Quarter Horse registration Number 1) are familiar to anybody who ever went to a stock show in Texas. At this writing, Hired Hand is still alive at the King Ranch at twenty-three and is still breeding sound.

Interestingly, Hired Hand was in the last crop of colts produced by Old Sorrel when the great sire was thirty years of age. Thus, Old Sorrel and Hired Hand together span more than half a century of horse breeding in but two horse generations.

Looking back, the King Ranch has but one or two regrets about Old Sorrel, Doctor Northway tells us. For one thing, nobody in those early days got around to taking pictures of the stallion in his prime. Or if they did, the photos are lost. We see him only as an aging horse, near the end of his career, a shadow of the great animal that commanded the admiration of men who had ridden thousands of good horses. It is unfortunate too that more precise breeding records aren't available now on every Old Sorrel cross. He was in his prime in the 1920s and 1930s, the Quarter Horse registry was not set up until 1940. So only his outstanding sons and daughters were chronicled and the later ones were assigned registration numbers. Old Sorrel himself became P-209.

Although we do not know exactly how many offspring Old Sorrel produced in his long life, (Foaled in 1915, he died in 1945) we do know that at least ninety-five per cent of the Quarter Horses on the King Ranch are Old Sorrel "top and bottom" in their pedigrees. The percentage may be closer to ninety-nine per cent, in the judgment of Doctor Northway.

Yet the ranch has not excluded all other blood. Some exceptional mares of other breeding are occasionally purchased. No outside stallions are brought in—although on occasion in past years such straight Thoroughbred sires as Chicaro and Lovely Manners were introduced into the program.

An outside mare today that comes to the King Ranch Quarter Horse program (There is a separate program for the breeding of Thoroughbred race horses) will follow a prescribed pattern: She will be bred to a direct descendant of Old Sorrel. If she produces a stud colt, the animal will be marked with an "X" on the right thigh and later gelded. If it is a filly, she too gets the "X" brand—but if she proves herself as a doing horse, she will later also be bred to direct Old Sorrel descendants. "You might call this an indirect outcross," says Doctor Northway.

On one point, we are told, there is no variation. Every mare, to become a broodmare, must prove herself as a working cow pony. The world may have changed in many ways and the cowhorse on today's King Ranch may be a vast improvement over the mount of the 1880s. Yet some things have not changed. To move cattle, you need a horse with "cow," one that will stop and turn and move, one with intelligence and good sense. Those are the qualities Captain King sought a century ago, qualities clearly defined by Bob Kleberg and Old Sorrel—and they are qualities western riders honor today.▲

10

PAINTED JOE

The Thoroughbred had its Byerly Turk.

The Quarter Horse had Peter McCue and Traveler.

The Paint Horse had Painted Joe as a foundation sire, known down through the years as adding both speed and quality to the individual Paints we have today.

Painted Joe, however, does not go back into the dim mists of time as does the progenitor of the Thoroughbred breed and some of the other foundation sires. The best-known Paint of them all — and Painted Joe doubtless qualifies for that description — was foaled in 1939 and lived two full decades. He died in 1959. Some of his offspring are still very much alive and active.

Perhaps the most fascinating initial discovery about Painted Joe is the apparent foul-up that has existed in his pedigree for most of the years since he became prominent. In researching the great stallion's background for its first stud book, the American Paint Horse Association established to its satisfaction that Painted Joe is not, as previously thought, by Joe Bailey, AQHA P-4, or even by a son of Joe Bailey. This is the pedigree that Painted Joe raced under in the 1940s while in the old American Quarter Horse Racing Association of Tucson, Arizona — and the pedigree by which most horsemen knew him. This Joe Bailey breeding went into the Quarter Horse Racing Association records as breeders registered Joe's sons and daughters.

Recently, however, the Paint Association contacted the man who bred Painted Joe — Owen E. Lay of Sealy, Texas — and obtained what it considers to be the accurate pedigree on Painted Joe.

"We have accepted Mr. Lay's pedigree of the horse," wrote Paint Association Executive Secretary Sam Spence, "and the only explanation we can give for this pedigree not being brought out sooner is simply that no one previously made the effort to consult the stallion's breeder . . ."

The true breeding of Painted Joe, Spence added, does not lessen either the racing or breeding accomplishments of the horse — what he did and the quality he sired speak for themselves.

"The APHA does feel, however, that for future records and reference purposes, it is important to know the correct breeding of this foundation Paint stallion."

Joe was foaled March, 1939, on Lay's ranch at Sealy, about thirty-five miles west of Houston. In the early 1920s a load of horses from the north country came into Sealy. Among them was a Paint stallion, eventually purchased by Mr. Lay and bred to his blaze-faced, stocking-legged race mare, Lizzy. The result was a predominantly-white Paint filly, which was never broke and never named. Early in 1938 this filly — now grown to be a mature mare — was bred to Mr. Lay's chestnut Quarter stallion, Rondo Joe. Thus, his sire was Rondo Joe, his dam the Paint mare who was by the Paint stallion and the running mare.

Rondo Joe was by Grano de Oro, one of the products of Ott Adams' South Texas cross of Little Joe and Della Moore, which also produced Joe Reed and Joe Moore. Rondo Joe's dam was a Hobbmaker mare by a son of Sykes Rondo, the old foundation Quarter Horse from Nixon, Texas.

Painted Joe was broke as a long yearling in 1940 on another of the Lay ranches at Luling, Texas, some ninety miles west of Sealy. "I tried to rope calves on him," Lay recalls, "but he was too rough in the chute and he'd run right over a calf."

Painted Joe, in this old and damaged photo, is shown to be no halter champion. Taken at the track, this picture shows him in lean, hard racing shape. His grooming then was not important. Reaching the finish line first was.

One day he remembers that a couple of friends came by his place to measure the stride on their race mare. "We opened her up on a dirt road and found she was striding twenty-two feet which really pleased her owners. I had been riding Painted Joe and after everyone left I slipped off his saddle and breezed him down the road. His stride measured exactly twenty-four feet . . . I knew then he could run a pretty good lick."

Lay's judgment was proved correct when he hauled the young stud around to some of the local areas and raced against everybody's roping horses.

"He ran off and left everything we matched him against even though we were just running short arena races," said Lay. He pointed out that probably ninety per cent of all these roping horses were sons and grandsons of Old Joe Bailey,

Painted Joe, Jr. (above) and Geranamo were two of Painted Joe's best-known colts. Joe, Jr., was said to have run AAA time at the age of sixteen. Unfortunately, he was gelded as a youngster. Geranamo stood for some years in Arizona as a prolific sire of Paints.

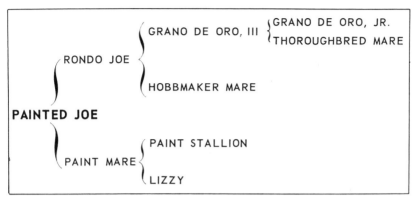

whose home was at Gonzales, Texas, just about eighteen miles south of Luling. This could well account for Painted Joe being mistakenly tagged with the Joe Bailey pedigree.

Early in 1941, Lay hauled Painted Joe to San Antonio where he made a deal with Boyd Givens to race the horse during his second year. In January of 1942 Givens bought the young Paint from Lay for $375. He immediately left for Tucson where he matched Painted Joe against—and outran—the famous "iron horse," Clabber. Within three weeks Givens had sold Painted Joe to Tom Clark of Tucson for $2,500.

It was Clark's turn to race the horse successfully. Then he sold him to Vernon Goodrich of Maxwell, New Mexico. Under the two owners, over a period of time, Painted Joe outran such Quarter Horse notables as Cowboy, Miss Banks, Squaw H., Chicaro, Clabber, Grey Badger II, Peaches, Sugar Foot, Arizona Girl, Bartender, Sleepy Joe, Duke, Blueberry Hill, Roman Sandals, Spotted Spider and Grey Hancock.

Painted Joe is officially listed in the *1945 Year Book* of the American Quarter Racing Association as a Register of Merit Quarter Running Horse. His best times are listed as: 220 yards—12.8; 300 yards—16.2; 330 yards—17.6; 350 yards—18.6; 400 yards—20.8; 440 yards—22.8.

In later years, Tom Clark bought Painted Joe back and then sold him to Dave Miller of Mammoth, Arizona. The grand old stallion died at the age of twenty in 1959 at Miller's ranch on the San Pedro River.

This brief outline of Joe's life barely touches on his racing career and does not include all of his owners. Another owner was John Janzen, who raced the stallion successfully and stood him at stud for several years near Enid, Oklahoma. Quarter and Paint Horse breeder Bob Sutherland of Kansas City, Missouri, recalls seeing Painted Joe at Enid in 1943. "He stood about fifteen hands and weighed some 1,200 pounds in running condition. He was without doubt one of the most beautiful and proud animals ever placed on this earth," recalls Sutherland. "The finest attribute is that Painted Joe passed these qualities on to his get."

He did indeed sire a lot of good running horses. Perhaps his greatest daughter is Babette, APHSA #1050. A 1944 foal, Babette chalked up an enviable record in the Quarter Running Association and went on to become an outstanding broodmare. One of her sons is registered today in the American Quarter Horse Association and has an official AA Register of Merit rating.

Two of Painted Joe's sons stand out, in terms of reputation, above the rest: Geronamo and Painted Joe, Jr.

Geronamo, APSHA #12, was raced for a number of years by his former owner, Art Pollard of Sonoita, Arizona. He was reportedly unbeaten in match races and stood "open to the world" for 220 yards. Geronamo is himself a noted sire of Paint Horses today.

Painted Joe, Jr., APSHA #1016, is a legend in his own time. This 1949-foaled gelding ran — in 1965 — in AAA time — and defeated several AAA-rated Quarter Horses. To say that it is rare for a fifteen-year-old horse to run AAA time is the understatement of the century. Owned by Cal Allison of Allen, Oklahoma, Painted Joe, Jr., still has the clean legs of a two-year-old and the conformation of a show horse. His feats on the brush tracks of Texas and Oklahoma would fill a volume by themselves. Many a racehorse breeder has mourned the fact that this exceptional horse was gelded.

Painted Joe sired many other outstanding mares and producers of fine horses registered in the American Paint Horse Association. His daughters are today highly-valued members of some of the nation's leading Paint broodmare bands. His reputation will continue to grow in importance in years to come—even as Traveler and Peter McCue blood have grown in importance among Quarter Horsemen—as a pedigree ingredient in producing not only good horses but fast ones. ▲

11

PETER McCUE

Dawn's crisp chill was still in the air as the little jockey settled his 113 pounds firmly in the irons. He braced the big bay stallion for a fast start. Down the track five men waited with stop watches poised.

It was a huge colt they were going to clock at a quarter of a mile. Long-bodied, he weighed more than 1,400 pounds as a two-year-old and few of the people who saw him expected any spectacular burst of speed in the short sprints.

But the jockey knew better. His name was Milo Burlingame, still in his teens this May morning of 1897, and he had ridden the great horse before and knew how he could fly at four furlongs. Burlingame had no gate this day—nor did he have any four-footed competition. The track was empty save only for the one horse.

His name: Peter McCue. His reputation: A better—than—average Thoroughbred sprinter, making the rounds of the midwestern tracks.

His destiny: To become one of the best-known foundation sires of the Quarter Horse breed.

But time was all that interested Peter McCue's jockey in 1897. He knew what the horse was capable of. Never, in the two races he had run at St. Louis, had another horse really extended Peter McCue or really made him go all out. So young Burlingame gathered the prancing animal, turned him down the dirt track—and seconds later, he recalled half a century later, "It was the closest to flying I have ever felt." Burlingame pushed his mount as hard as he could go. The owner wanted to know just how fast this horse *could* run for a quarter mile. And as he flashed past the clockers, they found out: twenty-one seconds—or less.

"When I had took him up and got back," the little jockey wrote in an article in 1947, "the five watches had been brought together, and I saw them all with his time on them, just as it was snapped as I got off. Two were under twenty-one seconds, and three were exactly twenty-one seconds . . . I can say quite honestly that I believe the watches of that morning were correct (they were all experienced race timers and handicappers) and that it was the fastest time for a quarter ever run from a score line . . .

"I feel sure," he added, "that it would be under twenty-two seconds from a gate in our day . . . "

Today's world racing record for the 440 sprint is 21.6 seconds.

Burlingame's story of that epic one-horse race against five stop watches was published first by the National Quarter Horse Breeders Association, Stud Book No. 1. It was among the earliest contributions to what has become a bulky file of controversy about the racing career and ancestry of Peter McCue. Over the years, Quarter Horsemen have been arguing about whether the quick bay horse was really a registered Thoroughbred (by the Duke of Highlands) or a Quarter Horse (by Dan Tucker). Some horsemen will tell you there has been about as much fiction contributed to the fuss as fact.

Every writer therefore faces the danger of perpetuating a myth when he tackles the Peter McCue story. However, since one of the horseman's favorite indoor sports (especially in winter time) is debating the pedigrees of long-dead horses, it is a hazard we can confront with some calm. And there is a large body of hard fact connected with Peter McCue.

There isn't much question but what this horse first saw the light of day February 23, 1895, at the Samuel Watkins farm near Petersburg, Illinois. This is historic country, only a few

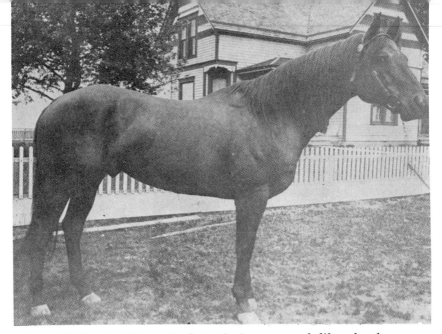

Peter McCue, in this early photo, looks very much like what he was —a racehorse of Thoroughbred breeding and of substantial size. He weighed more than 1,400 pounds as a two-year-old colt. But it now seems certain that his sire was Dan Tucker and not a Thoroughbred stallion. His dam was a half-Thoroughbred mare.

miles from New Salem where Abe Lincoln split rails and courted Ann Rutledge. President Andrew Jackson signed the land grant that gave Sam Watkins' father, Joseph, the homestead he developed into a prosperous farm. Sam and his wife raised eight children and he was a pillar of the community. This is to pin down the fact that the Watkins clan was solid and respectable and not old-time race track drifters or opportunists. They did, however, subscribe to one common practice of the day, concerning Thoroughbred horse registration, that set the stage for the Peter McCue debate. As explained by writer William Welch in *The Quarter Horse Journal* in 1946, Sam Watkins recorded Peter McCue in 1895 as a foal by his Thoroughbred stallion, Duke of Highlands. This was done in order that the horse could later race on recognized tracks. It was not to deceive buyers — who were told, reported Welch, that the young horse was actually by Sam Watkins' other stud, Dan Tucker.

As puzzling as this may seem today, it must be remembered that the breed registration standards in 1895 were not as strict as they are now and many breeders took liberties with registration unheard of a few decades later. At any rate, there was no question in the minds of the Watkins family but that Dan

Tucker, who was not a registered Thoroughbred, sired Peter McCue. Watkins' son William prepared a sworn affidavit on May 17, 1946, testifying to this. The younger man was on the farm at the time of the colt's birth and knew of his own personal knowledge, apparently, that Dan Tucker was the sire.

What makes the debate academic now is that *whichever* horse sired Peter McCue gave him plenty of running horse blood. His dam, Nora M, was at least half Thoroughbred. Her sire was the registered stud Voltigeur. And Dan Tucker was by Barney Owens out of a Jack Traveler mare. So if Peter McCue wasn't by the Duke of Highlands, he was still at least three-quarters Thoroughbred.

At this point, the novice horseman may ask: So what? Well, all this has been important to "short" horsemen down through the years because Peter McCue founded himself a virtual dynasty. It has been estimated that at *least three-fourths of all the Quarter Horses alive today can trace their ancestry to Peter McCue.* Small wonder that breeders have debated *his* ancestry.

At any rate, Peter McCue did come up with a bona fide Jockey Club number and to the world of the 1890s he was a Thoroughbred horse. At the age of two, a youngster named Dick Hornback is said to have broke and started the colt in training, riding the big animal prior to his going to the track. When time came for Peter McCue to make his track debut, Sam Watkins allowed a nephew, Charles Watkins to actually race the horse. It is ironic that Peter McCue never earned a dollar for his original owner. A dispute developed later between Sam and Nephew Charles and it took legal action for the elder Watkins to recover his horse.

Peter McCue's official racing record was also a matter of debate until 1951 when The American Quarter Horse Association commissioned Wayne Dinsmore, an authority on the subject, to check the available records. A detailed listing, first published by the AQHA in 1951, sets forth Peter McCue's entire documented career. There is little doubt that he also ran on some unrecognized tracks, possibly even in some quarter-mile races. However, Milo Burlingame's written recollections half a century later constitute the only eyewitness

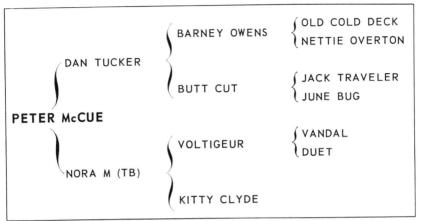

accounts we have of the horse in a carefully-clocked quarter mile race.

The chart, from *Goodwin's Turf Guides,* was compiled with help from the *Daily Racing Form* staff. It shows that Peter McCue had a reasonably good year as a two-year-old, with eight wins, one second and two thirds in sixteen starts. He did not do as well as a three-year-old. In twelve races, he won only one time, placed twice and was third three times. Six times he finished out of the money. The year 1899 found Peter McCue doing poorly with one second and a third in nine races. Owner Watkins felt the horse had been raced too hard and too often in his second year and, after legal action, recovered Peter McCue from his nephew.

This is when the horse was turned to stud. He was leased out in 1901 or 1902 for breeding to a man named Michaels in Logan County, Illinois. However, *The American Stud Book* shows twenty registered Thoroughbred mares sired by Peter McCue, the first one foaled in 1900. Which means Sam Watkins himself began breeding the horse in his fourth year. Records indicate that Peter McCue stayed in Illinois until 1907. Volume X of the Stud Book shows he had four Thoroughbred-registered female foals in 1901, three in 1902, one in 1903, three in 1904, two in 1905, two in 1907, three in 1908 and one in 1909. Those in 1908 and 1909 are shown to have been bred by John Wilkins of San Antonio, Texas. This presumably marks the transfer of Peter McCue to his first Texas home. He was to have two other owners in his lifetime, on the basis of available records — he was sold first to Milo Burlingame about 1911 and then Burlingame sold him to Si Dawson and Coke Roberds, about 1916.

Historically, we now enter the period when Peter McCue became a prolific sire of what was one day to be called the Quarter Horse. In the early days of this century many people referred to short-running horses as "Steel Dust" horses, after the famous sprinter of that name. But since most of the sprints were set up for a quarter-mile, the term "Quarter Horse" began to be popular. There was to be no official registry for this type until 1940, but horses like Peter McCue — crossed on some of the quick, tough little mustang mares of the southwest — now began to set the genetic stage for the new breed.

Milo Burlingame's experience may have been typical. His first intention was to get about five good Thoroughbred mares and breed only these to Peter McCue, since the horse was registered. "But I had a lot of friends," he wrote later, "and I would tell them to go breed to him..." Thus, the progeny of the big Illinois stud began to spread across cow country. Soon, horses like John Wilkins, Harmon Baker, Badger, A. D. Reed, Jack McCue, Chief, Buck Thomas, Sheik and Hickory Bill began to be talked about. Over the years these sons of Peter McCue were to insure his equine immortality. Take Hickory Bill, for example. He sired Old Sorrel — and if he had stopped right there, it would have been enough to secure his place in horse history. Old Sorrel became the foundation sire sire of all King Ranch breeding. Consider the tens of thousands of Quarter Horses bred on the King Ranch since the ranch acquired Old Sorrel from George Clegg in 1916 — every one traced its pedigree directly to Peter McCue through Hickory Bill, not one time but repeatedly.

Peter McCue's other sons and daughters produced families equally well-known in the Southwest. From Badger came the great Midnight stallion — through him the noted Grey Badger II (by Midnight, Jr.) and Waggoner and Chubby. Harmon Baker was another potent son of Peter McCue, producing Dodger, who in turn sired Pretty Boy and Talley Man. From Pretty Boy came the modern sire Pretty Buck. Jazz, another of Peter McCue's good sons, was the grandsire of the immortal cutting

*One of Peter McCue's noted sons was Badger. That stallion pro-
duced a famed family of his own, including such good descendants
as Grey Badger II, through Midnight and Midnight, Jr.*

champion, Jessie James. Chief sired Peter McCue, Jr., while
Sheik was the sire of Nick, who produced Nick Shoemaker and
by him, Spanish Nick. The John Wilkins stud sired Joe Hancock and through him, Roan Hancock.

It is important to note here that the offspring of Peter
McCue, aside from founding their own families, produced both
running champions and arena performance champions. In 1957,
for instance, *The Quarter Horse Journal* produced male line
descent charts of the major Quarter Horse families—and it
showed Peter McCue leading the field in both the number of
sires of AQHA Champions (forty-three), and the number of
broodmare sires of AQHA Champions (forty-three). The next
closest horse was Traveler (thirty and thirteen). Among race-

horse sires, Peter McCue ranked fifth that year with thirty-three of his descendants having run AAA time.

Perhaps because so many of his descendants became great performance champions, the notion has spread that Peter McCue was the early ideal of Quarter Horse conformation. Certainly we do hear today any number of Quarter Horsemen talking about the need to "keep the real, old-fashioned, honest-to-goodness Quarter Horses like Peter McCue." It seems possible that a lot of owners have the impression that this horse was the Compleat Stock Horse, a model we can still breed toward. Was he a Quarter Horse, as we know one today? Hardly. By modern standards, Peter McCue could not be held up as any conformation ideal. He had a good head and good withers. Muscle, yes. But we would fault him on his bulk, his length of back, perhaps — unless the cameras distort him — on his neck. But anybody who sneers and says, "That old horse wouldn't stand a chance in a halter class *now*!" misses the more important point. Peter McCue, like Old Fred and Traveler and others, was a Thoroughbred-type horse that, when crossed on good native mares, produced the stock horse we are so proud of today. Peter McCue's fame rests not on his racing record or his ancestry. It rests, instead, on the fact that he passed his speed, his strength and his capacity to reproduce quality on to scores of his descendants, both male and female. This is what produced the chain reaction of good breeding that continues to this day. ▲

12

STEEL DUST

Eleven o'clock was the time set for the race. But nobody moving around McKinney's town square figured the race could start on schedule.

It couldn't and it didn't. And no wonder. Wagons and horses by the twos and threes were still bringing people into town from all over north Texas. Some, from distant settlements like Jefferson in east Texas, had spent days on the trail, to see this horse race. And most knew they would have to camp out when they arrived.

McKinney, Texas, on September 5, 1856, could not handle much of a crowd. It's one tiny hostel, the Foote House, had only four rooms—yet thirty-two women had bedded down there the night before. Their husbands and other visitors either found beds in the village's twenty-seven houses or in the board front stores around the square—or out under the stars.

Excitement generated by Sunday's big race was exceeded only by the betting it generated. Suddenly the town—or most of it, anyway—had a home-grown champion. And as McKinney's population swelled from less than 500 to more than 2,000, it was a cautious man indeed who could resist the impulse to make a small wager.

Most McKinney residents, of course, favored Harrison Stiff's local horse, a big, bay stallion named Monmouth. He *looked* like a racehorse and he was. High-strung, standing over sixteen hands, he was far and away the favorite.

The other horse was a slate gray color (today he might be called a grulla) with a dorsal stripe down the back. His handlers called him Steel Dust. He was twelve years old, appeared to be some fifteen hands in height—and also appeared to have a bit of a problem staying awake. With his head drooping and with a little of his age beginning to show, he simply did not look like he was in Monmouth's league at all.

And yet Steel Dust's owners—Middleton Perry and Jones Greene—had not made that long trek from down at Lancaster, Texas, fifty odd miles away, just for the exercise. Their stallion was preceded by his reputation. It was reported that he had beaten everything on the Texas frontier. Except Monmouth, that is. And the Monmouth backers bet their cash, some bet horses, some cows, saddles, bridles, even wagons, on the outcome.

The word had been out for months about this race. In an era when horse racing was the biggest (almost the *only*) outdoor sport in Texas, this was a dream match for every man who figured he knew something about horses. And every man then figured as how he did. Which meant he would back his judgment with something negotiable.

The Lancaster entry and his backers got into McKinney on Friday night and Monmouth's owner generously provided space for Steel Dust in his stable. Neither contingent took any chances. Both horses were well guarded night and day against any shenanigans.

Some protection for humans was in order too. Whiteley's Saloon could not handle the flow of customers Sunday as race time approached. Whiteley kept seven bartenders busy carrying drinks out on the square. We are also advised by one McKinney chronicler that hotel-owner Foote broke open a barrel of whiskey on the porch of a neighbor's log cabin home and sold it for a quarter a shot. Which resulted, sad to say, in some of the more ardent fans missing the race.

Sheriff James H. Lovejoy policed the situation well, apparently, because the pre-race festivities were free of vio-

When the future Texas governor waved his hat, it kicked off the most celebrated horse race in early Texas frontier history. The smaller of the two horses was to become legendary for helping to establish a breed in his own likeness. Distance for the race was a half mile and it started on a slight downhill slope.

lence. The good sheriff himself demonstrated sporting instincts and remarked to Jordon O. Straughan, "Well, Jordon, I'm laying every cent I can rake up on old Monmouth. Look at him! You think that horse can't run?"

The Sheriff and most every other man in town had watched the Saturday pre-race workouts on the race track just northwest of town. It did seem to some, though, that the Negro boy riding Steel Dust (Tom MacKnight) was holding the stallion back somewhat.

At about 1:30 p.m. on the afternoon of September 5, a huge crowd lined the race course, virtually emptying the town. It is doubtful whether so many people had ever witnessed a single match race on the Texas frontier, up to that time.

To fully appreciate this turnout, it must be remembered that in 1856 both Lancaster and McKinney were as large if not larger than the village of Dallas. The census of 1850 shows them bigger. Suiting the occasion, the race people in McKinney had cleared a straightaway track a full mile in length. Since McKinney is in rolling country, the track went down one slope, up another, then down a gentle incline to the finish. But the matchmakers found they couldn't race for a mile. Monmouth was a miler but Steel Dust was a quarter miler. They compromised on a half-mile race.

It was to start on the first rise of ground and the last quarter mile followed roughly the course of present day Tucker Street, through what is now a residential section of McKinney. The finish line was set up near the east end of Tucker, where today it turns into Broad Street.

The only surviving eyewitness account of the race itself comes from George A. Wilson, an early-day settler, as reported many years later by a McKinney historian, Captain Roy Hall. Wilson stood at the finish line, he told Hall, and recalled:

"*There were not over 5,000 people in Collin County but I believe twice that many were present . . . Men, women and children, Negroes and Indians, and everybody had a bet up. We could see the starting point through the trees and saw Jim (J.W. Throckmorton, later governor of Texas) wave his black hat to start them off.*

"*They came down off the hill neck and neck and disappeared from sight in Williams Draw. People yelled, shouted, and women and boys started to climb trees to get a view of the horses — but before they got up the racers came up over the rise.*

"*Big Monmouth was taking gigantic strides but the little mousey horse was making two jumps to old Monmouth's one. They were not long strides but he was making them faster.*

"*Steel Dust was on the left with the little Negro boy lying squat down on his back. Bob (Rudolph) was thrashing Monmouth but I could not see that the Negro boy was doing anything to Steel Dust. Before we could think, they were at the finish line, Steel Dust three lengths in front. Steel Dust turned sharp off the track and plowed to a stop. Old Monmouth kept right on and ran into the thicket, sweeping Bob off his back (the riders rode bare-*

*back) and disappearing from view, crashing off down in
the woods.*

*"I think everybody in the county lost something,"
Wilson continued. "I was lucky. I only bet a pair of sad-
dlebags but John (possibly his friend, John Kincaid) lost
a cow and a mule. There was a heap of cutting up in
town that night, but mostly by the Dallas crowd. Most of
us slunk off home, poorer but wiser."*

It is not reported just how much money Steel Dust won for
Greene and Perry and their associates. But certainly it was a
small disaster for Collin County. We can imagine the household discussions that took place between pioneer wives and
husbands that night after the race. Possibly it is not significant but no history of the county or city has yet turned up
which even mentions the race. Monday, September 7, 1856,
could hardly have been anything but a black day in McKinney.

By contrast, the jubilation at Lancaster—now largely a
residential community thirteen miles south of Dallas—was
lasting. Steel Dust was a celebrity. And the only person there
who may have felt anything but pure joy at the victory could
have been thirteen-year-old James Henry Ellis. Young Henry
had worked Steel Dust for months before the race in the pasture across the road from the Ellis homestead. (It still stands
in much of its original condition.) He had cared for the animal,
exercised him, planned to ride him in the McKinney race. He
even had his racing outfit sewn together. And then his good
church-going mother discovered that the race was scheduled
for the Sabbath. That ripped it—and Henry was an ex-jockey.

"Father was disappointed," recalled his daughter, Mrs.
Ethel Scott, in 1967. "He rode Steel Dust in his training and
planned on riding him in the race." Henry lived to be eighty-
seven years old and his children became familiar with the
circumstances of the famed contest.

The Ellises and Greenes and Perrys were closely linked
in the story of Steel Dust. Today their many descendants recall childhood stories told them by elders of the frontier days.
They were hardy types, those early settlers, and they produced

a lot of vigorous people. Nearly all who survived infancy, one gathers, lived amazingly long lives. Some of the original settlers lived well into their nineties. Children of those original settlers of the 1840s still live in the same communities of north Texas. They remember with complete clarity how their parents looked, talked and details of personality.

Which makes for a real puzzle in the Steel Dust saga. Despite detailed knowledge of the people, we have almost no documentation on Steel Dust's life. Yet so widespread was his reputation clear into the 20th century that the term "Quarter" Horse was not as often used, apparently, as the term "Steel Dusts"—in referring to short-coupled, stock or racing-type western horses. Like Justin Morgan, he gave his name to a whole new breed.

Many oldtimers who grew up on western ranges in the early years of the 20th century never knew for sure, in fact, whether any such horse as Steel Dust actually ever lived. They thought the term referred to a color or a type of horse, rather than any particular animal.

The absence of Steel Dust factual data—breeding records, sales contracts or publicity—can be traced to the character of the times. Some of the early settlers were simple, uneducated men. Some could not read or write. Many never had to sign their names but once or twice in a lifetime. They were ambitious, courageous and courteous—but formal education was something they later provided for their children.

Had it not been for a few early writers and researchers like Bob Denhardt, Helen Michaelis and Wayne Gard, the story of Steel Dust might have been lost to us. Beginning in the 1930s they and a few others began sifting fact from fancy. And fancy there was plenty of. It was hard to find a horse in Texas whose owner did not claim that he was a direct descendant of Steel Dust.

This much of Steel Dust's early life and times seems to be authenticated: When Jones Greene and Middleton Perry loaded their families and worldly belongings into wagons and set out for Texas in 1844, Steel Dust went also. He was a yearling, having been foaled in 1843 in Kentucky. The trek began from Kane, Illinois, roughly fifty miles north of St. Louis. Greene's and Perry's wives were sisters of the Ellis family, Mary Witt

```
                                                    ┌ BLACKBURN'S WHIP
                              ┌ SHORT'S WHIP     ┤
                              │                     ┤
              ┌ HARRY BLUFF  ┤
              │               │                     ┌ TIMOLEON
              │               └ BIG NANCE (TB)   ┤
    STEEL DUST                                      ┤
              │
              │
              └ UNKNOWN
```

and Ellen Malinda. Their father and the rest of the Ellis clan were to follow them to Texas after they had found the ideal place to settle.

Steel Dust's family tree, as researched by the late Helen Michaelis and Bob Denhardt, goes back to some of the most distinguished Thoroughbred breeding of early America. It does at least on the sire's side. Steel Dust's sire was Harry Bluff by Short Whip. Harry Bluff was out of the Thoroughbred mare, Big Nance—who was by Timoleon by Sir Archy. Pedigree followers will recognize in Sir Archy one of the most prolific and important of the Colonial period sires. We know nothing, however, of Steel Dust's dam. He does not appear to have been registered as a Thoroughbred horse.

T he Perrys and Greenes settled on Ten Mile Creek just below Lancaster, Texas, then a settlement called Hard Scrabble. Writing in 1959, Wayne Gard (*Fabulous Quarter Horse: Steel Dust; Duell, Sloan and Pierce, New York*) described that community as "two rows of hastily-built log cabins with chimneys of sticks and mud." It was a wild land, raided occasionally by roving bands of Indians yet full of game for the eating and good, black land for the plowing. Each family acquired 640 acres—as did the Ellis family when it arrived two years later.

Steel Dust quickly grew into a distinctive horse, both in conformation and speed. Mature, he stood just over fifteen hands and weighed, by all accounts, 1,200 pounds. He was a short-coupled Thoroughbred type of horse—seemingly of the "middle of the road" type Quarter Horse today. His descendants tell much about Steel Dust's muscling. They are described as having the short backs and deep barrel of the future Quarter Horse, the bulging jaw and little sharp ear, the heavier muscles in the forearm and the overall compactness that tells of quick speed and "action."

By the time Steel Dust was a fully-grown stallion, his speed in the Lancaster area was well-known and neighbors had started breeding good mares to him. Undoubtedly, many brought their best running-type mares. Men in those days, as today, wanted to own a fine racehorse. But many others bred common mares, probably even some mustang mares to Steel Dust. In what numbers we don't know. But the horse undoubtedly produced nearly a decade of colt crops in the Lancaster area before he gained renown throughout the frontier with his famous win over Monmouth.

This came near the end of his racing career and was all the more impressive because of his age. Few stallions today still race at twelve. Yet there were still two more well-chronicled high points in Steel Dust's running career. One involved the stallion, Brown Dick, owned by a neighbor of the Greenes and Perrys, Alfred Bailes.

Another running horse man near Lancaster, Jack Batchler, borrowed Steel Dust from the owners for this race. And although Brown Dick had never lost a race—so we are told—he lost that one. And Steel Dust's fame went even farther along the frontier.

Despite Jack Batchler's respect for Steel Dust's speed, he felt that he personally had more than a match for the horse in an animal named Shiloh. Here is another name that looms large in the early mists of Quarter Horse history. Shiloh has a far better documented pedigree and a better-chronicled history than Steel Dust.

Shiloh was foaled in Tennessee about 1844 by Union by Von Tromp by Thomas' Big Solomon by Sir Solomon by the noted Sir Archy—which made him and Steel Dust distant relatives. Shiloh was an impressive animal, described by some horsemen as the finest they had even seen. Batchler, who made a part of his living from racing and horses, was a sound judge of horseflesh and in his considered opinion, here was the horse to beat Steel Dust.

So a match was arranged at a short track just east of Dallas. As in the McKinney race, much of the community closed up shop to see the contest. Even the Dallas saloons closed down briefly. Lines of poles had been set up, through which the horses were to jump away from the starting line. And a son of Jack Batchler, Henry—a boy of seven at the time—is quoted by Wayne Gard in this description of what happened:

"Steel Dust was so eager for the show that he reared and plunged all the time he was in the chute. When he made his leap to clear the stall, he struck the wall and ran a splinter into his shoulder, which disabled him. Father galloped Shiloh over the track and claimed the forfeit, to which the judges decided he was entitled. As a result of the injury to his shoulder, Steel Dust went blind and never raced again."

That, in a few words, reports an end to the great horse's racing career. There is little documentation of Steel Dust's remaining life. One entry has turned up in Jack Batchler's studbook. A notation for April, 1864, records the fact that at the age of twenty, Steel Dust was still alive and in breeding condition. "... bred big fily to Stele Dust," Batchler wrote.

An honor roll of his famous offspring helps somewhat to fill in the historical blanks. The owners of both Steel Dust and Shiloh prospered from their lands and livestock. They bred Steel Dust fillies to Shiloh and Shiloh fillies to Steel Dust. The two stallions are so closely intertwined in many a modern short horse pedigree that some famed recent animals go back to the old horses two and three times on both top and bottom sides. Here are some of the Steel Dust get on which breeding records are thought to be accurate:

Tom Driver — This son of Steel Dust was out of a Shiloh filly. Tom Driver was the sire of Shelby who in turn sired Pid Hart, the sire of Rocky Mountain Tom.

Grey Alice — Possibly Steel Dust's most famous running daughter, this mare's race with Hildreth's Red Morocco is chronicled by Sam Hildreth in "The Spell of the Turf," published at Philadelphia in 1926.

Jack Traveller — He was a prime link between Steel Dust and Peter McCue, one of the best-known Quarter Horse foundation sires. Jack Traveller (sometimes spelled with one "l") sired Butt Cutt, Peter McCue's granddam through Dan Tucker. Jack Traveller also sired such producing daughters as Kiddy Waddle, Bird and Belle H. It is through registered Thoroughbred horses like Belle H, a brown mare, foaled in 1887, and listed in the *American Stud Book* that we are able to pin down some of the early breeding of Steel Dust horses. She shows up in Volume VII, page 1205.

Ram Cat — Another daughter of Steel Dust, she too was bred to Shiloh and produced, among others, the noted sire Old Billy who founded a complete family of his own. Whalebone by Old Billy in turn laid the foundation for the entire Rondo family of horses. Whalebone sired Lock's Rondo—one of the direct ancestors of King P-234.

Bill Fleming — He sired 80 Grey and June Grey. The latter was the dam of Ace of Hearts and 80 Grey was one of the most famous West Texas racehorses in the 1890s.

There are a host of others — including Old Rebel, Black George, John Cook, Bill Garner, Alice May, Mollie, Big Casino, Judy Mounts Steel Dust—Steel Dust contributed heavily to all the early prominent Quarter Horse families, especially Old Billy, Cold Deck, Rondo, Peter McCue and Joe Bailey strains.

From a practical standpoint, of course, the Steel Dust blood was only as good as the way it was crossed—which is true of any stallion. What made the Steel Dust strain so important to the early, formative years of the Quarter Horse was that his ability to produce both fast and well conformed "short" horses established a distinct type of horse, different from the pure Thoroughbred.

As this type emerged, Steel Dust also produced a small army of cavalry horses for the Civil War — and spread his breeding in the process. Mid Perry was one of those called to the Confederate colors in 1862. He formed a company of cavalry which served mostly in Arkansas and Lancaster residents say most of the Texans went to war on Steel Dust and Shiloh horses.

Will Williams, a son of Confederate veteran C. A. (Alex) Williams, wrote in 1940: "When my father joined the cavalry for war service, he went in with John Reynolds, later of Young County. They both rode Steel Dust colts, with much pride . . . Whenever they happened to get with another command of the army, the first thing they would do would be to match in quarter races. They said they had more money than they could spend . . ."

McKinney, Texas, at the time of the Steel Dust–Monmouth contest, was a frontier village of only a few dozen buildings. This photo, taken after the Civil War, shows its rapid growth as the southwest expanded. Horse racing then was the major outdoor sport and one on which nearly every Texas male considered himself an authority.

Not all the Lancaster horses made it home. Some were lost, some stolen, some captured.

In the post-war era, ranchers discovered that their Steel Dust-bred horses had more than cavalry and race track potential. Crossed with any kind of quality animals, they produced a sensible, fast, tough cowhorse—the kind a cowboy could depend on for a hard day's work. In the southwestern cow country, then beginning to open up, this kind of horse was in demand. This breeding objective, by many ranchers in many areas, it is now clear, led to the Quarter Horse that we know today.

By the first years of the 20th century, a Steel Dust type of horse was a well-established horse in nearly every part of the western range. Doctor J. K. Northway, longtime veterinarian at the big King Ranch in south Texas, recalls hearing much about Steel Dust horses in his youth.

"I remember as a child," he says, "my father bought Steel Dust horses from around Cotulla. They ran from chestnut to light chestnut. Many were light-colored on the underbelly and chest and feathered off light from the knees down. Some had a light nose. My father got them because they were more versatile. You could pull a buggy with them, plow a field or anything. They'd run from fourteen to 14.3."

As for Steel Dust himself, his final years are cloaked in silence. His owner's descendants are sure that his remains lie somewhere along the wooded reaches of Ten Mile Creek where he lived all his life. In his 1959 book, Author Gard tells of reports that the aging and blind old horse may have been sold to other owners. Obviously, only very hard times following the Civil War could have caused the Greenes and Perrys to part with the famed horse, if in fact they did. We prefer to think that Steel Dust lived into the 1870s on the same pasture he first knew as a yearling—honored, well-fed and continuing to produce prototypes of a great breed to come. ▲

13

TOP DECK

As colts will, the brown colt walked up behind the broodmare as she nursed her foal. And as mares will, she kicked at the intruder. Most times, such a reflex gesture on the part of a mare simply shoos a stray colt back to its mother. In this particular case, the mare connected and the brown colt limped away.

She had caught him just above the left knee. There was no fracture and the skin was not broken. Yet the blow was to trouble the colt for the remainder of his life. It kept him from ever racing—and may have had something to do with this colt becoming one of the best-known stallions in America.

Named Top Deck, he got his injury soon after he was foaled at the King Ranch in 1945. So slight did it appear at first glance that the young Thoroughbred seemed destined to follow in the footsteps of his illustrious sire, Equestrian. But the injury made itself apparent when, as an eighteen-month-old colt, Top Deck began his race training.

Doctor J. K. Northway remembers the case well. "It is difficult to say just why lameness persisted and plagued this horse," Doctor Northway wrote the writer recently. But it did bother the colt every time he bore down on this foot. This was doubtless a source of frustration to those who admired the colt's clean lines, muscling and speed. In his early sprints, despite the lameness, he demonstrated a speed potential that measured up to his distinguished forebears.

Equestrian, his sire, was by Equipoise out of a Man-O-War mare. *Frillery, the grandam of Equestrian, goes back to the great family of Fair Play and Broomstick. Equestrian was obtained from the Whitney family of eastern racing fame, grew into a beautiful horse and a fine stud. Top Deck's dam, River Boat by Chicaro, may have been the pedigree element that ultimately made Top Deck so potent in the "short" running field.

Chicaro, by imported *Chicle, would seem to suggest the long distance abilities of that family. "No one," says Doctor Northway, "knows yet just why Chicaro had the ability of producing a lot of early speed — or 'early foot,' as a horseman says — in his progeny, but they were very popular because of their ability to run and win short races..."

This is the only clue the pedigree enthusiast might find in Top Deck's background to forecast his astonishing career. Certainly he had no racing future. His *only* future — if he had one at all — was in the stud. By forcing him into breeding service as a young horse, the injury may well have thrust Top Deck into the Quarter Horse world where, as a registered Thoroughbred, he probably would never otherwise have trespassed.

He found his way into that world through Ernest Lane and J. B. (Johnny) Ferguson. Lane of Odom, Texas, was given the colt as a gift by the King Ranch bossman, Bob Kleberg.

If anybody could do something with the brown colt, Kleberg may have figured, it was his longtime friend Lane. A noted roper, rancher and racehorse breeder, Lane "liked the colt mighty well" when he got him. An operation on the colt's left knee did not, however, remedy the lameness there and he could not take race training.

So, as a two-year-old, Top Deck was bred to a few mares. One of the first was a compact Quarter-type race mare Johnny Ferguson sent over to Lane, name of Skippy F. She had a Thoroughbred sire and an unknown dam. But it turned out that Skippy could produce like a giant, particularly when bred to Top Deck. Her first Top Deck colt, foaled July 22, 1948, was named Star Deck F. That filly was destined to win the first Texas Futurity at Del Rio, Texas, in 1950. Skippy's "second

Top Deck, in 1960, at left, was at the peak of his breeding ability and his colts—including Go Man Go, at right—were famous for their running and breeding too. Yet the Quarter Horse world did not really beat a path to his door until he was moved to Oklahoma that year.

home'' got to be Lane's place and she produced, by the same sire, Skippy's Baby, Music Lover, Clear Deck, Mr. Kip, Janon and Skip Deck. All developed into AAA racehorses.

It did not take Ferguson of Wharton, Texas, long to get the race fever. He had been breeding Quarter Horses for some years and liked to produce the kind that would work cattle as well as run. His operation would continue to produce useful, working Quarter Horses. But Skippy F. and Top Deck began his real career as a short horseman. And as if Skippy hadn't done a good enough job for him, Ferguson happened upon Lightfoot Sis. He paid $300 for her in Louisiana. Three-quarters Thoroughbred, she seemed perfectly arranged to complement Top Deck's breeding and conformation. From her second trip to Top Deck, Lightfoot Sis foaled a sleek little speedster whose very name raises visions of an excited rooter on the rail: Go Man Go. This youngster, foaled in 1953, demonstrated early that he was really lightning in a colt suit. As a two-year-old, Go Man Go won nine out of ten starts, finishing second the other time. Nine of those starts were run in AAA time. He won ten of thirteen starts the following year — and in all thirteen races he covered the distances in AAA time. In 1955 he became the first two-year-old to be named a World Champion in the Quarter Horse breed. In 1956 the same honor was bestowed upon him and he became the first stallion to be so named twice. Again, in 1957, he was named a champion — this time the title was World's Champion Quarter Running Horse and Champion Stallion, putting him two up on any other Quarter Horse. His dam, Lightfoot Sis, ultimately produced five AAA offspring for Ferguson.

The event which captured the American public's attention, however, came in 1957 on a Saturday afternoon at Ruidoso, New Mexico, when Go Man Go was entered in a 440 sprint. Jockey Robert Strauss pushed the four-year-old stud across the finish line a full length ahead of Vannevar to slice one-tenth of a second off the existing world's record. Go Man Go had done the 440 in 21.8 seconds and he promptly became known the nation over as "The World's Fastest Quarter Horse." The record was to stand for years and it immediately focused horse industry attention on Go Man Go's sire. Was he producing any more like this?

Yes, matter of fact he was. He *had* been for some time. Johnny Ferguson, after breeding mares to Top Deck at Lane's place for some seven years decided he had to own that stud. In 1954 he made a deal to pay Lane $20,000 for the horse. Strangely, though, the world did not promptly beat a path to Ferguson's Wharton ranch. It was hard to understand. In 1954 Ferguson could — and did — advertise that Top Deck had produced such AAA offspring as Star Deck F., Magnolia Skipper, Amber Star, Mackay Boy, Moon Deck, Mackay Jimmie, Ridge Butler and Miss Mackay, along with an impressive list of good AA horses.

Also Top Deck sired outstanding colts from other people's great mares — as witness Eagle Top from the exceptional old producer, Eagle Call. Yet between 1954 and 1959, Ferguson found his Texas neighbors lukewarm to Top Deck breeding. Only a few of the really fine mares came to the stallion and there wasn't a year when his breeding volume, even at a $500 fee, was what it should have been.

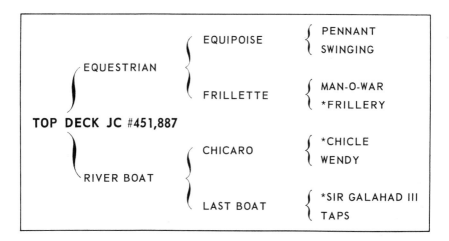

Finally Ferguson had to admit he was stumped. "I couldn't get the mares to him here. What's more, I'd breed a mare for $500 and almost have a lawsuit to collect the breeding fee... from friends! I don't know... maybe people wanted to have to travel a thousand miles to a stud... maybe he was too easy to find. But I couldn't get anything done."

At any rate, in 1960 Ferguson leased the horse to A. B. Green of Purcell, Oklahoma, the agreement being they would share in the breeding fees. And sure enough, Top Deck immediately became a more profitable investment. His stud fee went to $1,000 and his book was full that first year in Oklahoma. Later, it would go to $2,500, finally up to $3,500.

Along the way Top Deck's noted son, Go Man Go, stirred up a heated controversy within the American Quarter Horse Association. Then, as now, there were two schools of thought regarding the infusion of Thoroughbred blood into the Quarter Horse. Many stock horse breeders argue that such blood changes the entire character of the breed and makes a mockery of the idea of producing fine cowhorse types. Breeders like Ferguson on the other hand respect the cowhorse but see no reason why a judicious choice of short-running Thoroughbred blood cannot help the breed.

Said Ferguson: "I resent it when we Quarter Horse breeders are accused of breeding 'hot' Thoroughbred blood into the Quarter Horse. He (Top Deck) did not have it. What they're referring to was that back in the old remount days the government almost ruined a lot of ranches around the country by

113

loaning us long-legged, idiotic Thoroughbred-type studs...and we were supposed to produce cowhorses from them.

"The horses we are thinking about in the Top Deck type are short-backed with intelligent heads, lots of muscle where it belongs and the disposition we want..."

This honest difference of viewpoints made it difficult for Go Man Go, for one, to get a Quarter Horse registration number. Some breeders who opposed giving him a number argued that he was seven-eighths Thoroughbred. How could he be a Quarter Horse? Before the years-long controversy simmered down, a procedure had been worked out within the Quarter Horse association whereby Thoroughbred breeding — with extensive performance and inspection safeguards — could be admitted to Quarter Horse registration. And Go Man Go did eventually become #82,000 in the AQHA registry.

Then he broke into national renown once more when a new record price was recorded for his purchase. The event began one night at the Green Parrot Restaurant in Houston as the Frank Vessels and Bill Peckham families were eating dinner. Talk about the "great horses" of the breed soon brought the two men's attention to Go Man Go. Both allowed as how they'd love to own such a horse. The elder Vessels grinned and said he'd just like to *ride* him one time, to say that he'd *done* it!

But it didn't look like Go Man Go could be bought. Les Gosselin of Oklahoma City now had the young stud and Peckham was told he wasn't for sale. A month or so later, though, Vessels and Gosselin made an agreement which in turn made news. The purchase price was announced as $125,000, a new all-time record for a Quarter Horse to that time. (Actually, Peckham remembers the price as $120,000 plus some mares and the honoring of prior breeding contracts. These contracts, later purchased back by Peckham and Vessels, may have run the total consideration up possibly as high as $150,000.)

This sale, publicized widely, was a high-voltage shot in the arm for the Quarter Horse. Millions of people suddenly found out there was such a breed and what they were used for. Within the western horse industry, Top Deck breeding took on a new distinction. It began to pay off at both the track and the auction ring.

A. B. Green and Ferguson became partners on Top Deck in July, 1962, when the Oklahoman purchased a one-half interest in the stud. The price was not made public. An increasing flow of Top Deck colts to tracks in New Mexico and California quickly put the stallion in the front rank of breeding demand. Four and then five-figure selling prices for Top Deck offspring became common at Quarter Horse sales.

The now-famous All-American race at Ruidoso — set for its fourth running in 1962 — also quickened the pace of Top Deck's snowballing reputation. Total purse for the All-American that year was $222,850, and Johnny Ferguson left the track that afternoon richer by $96,425. His Hustling Man colt, by Go Man Go, had whipped the field in the 400 yard classic.

Next year saw another Top Deck-bred two-year-old run off with the All-American. This time it was Hugh Huntley from California who took home most of the marbles ($127,500) as his Goetta filly, also by Go Man Go, beat all the rest. It was an own daughter of Top Deck, Decketta, who won the All-American in 1964, earning $134,030 for owner W. W. Wilson of Oklahoma.

And if anybody was still skeptical about the short-running ability of the Top Decks after the 1964 All-American they kept their opinions to themselves. Incredibly enough, four of the first six colts to finish the 400 in that race — for a total purse of $302,060 — were get or grand get of Top Deck! It was the most complete domination of the richest racing prize in the world that had taken place. Here is how they finished:

1. Decketta by Top Deck
2. Steam Go Go by Go Man Go
3. Merry Go by Go Man Go
4. Tonto Parr
5. Hankins' Bars
6. Go Harriett by Go Man Go

By 1967, Top Deck and his family — along with Three Bars and *his* descendants — dominated both the records and the prices paid for running Quarter Horses in this country. Of the seventy-seven running Quarter Horses entered in the All-American futurity in September, 1967, no less than thirty-six had some Top Deck breeding. In the sixth All-American year-ling sale that accompanied the big race, 170 young running Quarter Horse prospects were sold. A total of fifty-one were of Top Deck breeding. They alone brought a whopping $197,-550 or an average of $3,873.

The year 1966 saw Top Deck at the top of the Quarter Horse breed's list of leading sires of race winners. His colts led the 1966 totals in number of wins, number of winners and starts. A total of fifty-four Top Deck colts were winners and they won 133 times. Three Bars was second that year with forty-seven winners and 121 wins. Go Man Go by Top Deck was third in this ranking with ninety-nine wins by thirty-six winners.

Still others of his sons showed promise of continuing his line — and the market for his blood. Names like Go Man Go, Moon Deck, Top Bracket, Top Flight, Top Decker, Mr. Mackay and a host of others assure a future for the kind of sprint Thoroughbred breeding that, controversial or not, is here to stay in the Quarter Horse business.

As for the old horse himself, Top Deck died at the pinnacle of his success. Not long after he passed his twentieth birth-day in 1965 he developed what appeared to be a kidney ail-ment. The best specialists were brought in but Top Deck could not be saved. He died September 24, 1965, and was buried at the A. B. Green Ranch, called Green Pastures, near Purcell, Oklahoma.

Possibly the most succinct epitaph Top Deck might have came from Doctor Northway at the King Ranch. He gave the writer a detailed five generation pedigree of the horse. Be-neath it, in what must be a classic of understatement, Top Deck was described thus:

"Injured from kick of mare in pasture when a foal — result: deformed left knee. Did not race. Very successful in the stud."▲

14

TRAVELER

Chilled to the bone, Chris Seale was glad to get back to town — even though Baird, Texas, in the 1890s didn't offer much luxury to either horse or rider.

A drizzling rain had nearly drenched him through as he rode down Baird's main street and got off his horse in front of Brown Seay's two-story, brick hotel. Inside it was warm and as he peeled off his wet garments, he reflected on his trip out beyond the edge of town.

A man would have to be mighty silly, he doubtless smiled to himself, to go out in this weather just to look at a horse. But that's what Seay had asked him to do and rancher Seale did it gladly—even though some might consider it sort of unusual. Seale had gone to the camp of Triggerfoot Self to see an old stud Self had brought to town.

Self had been around town for a few days talking about a fast horse he had—a chestnut sorrel stallion, maybe eight, ten years old. Self got the horse from a Texas & Pacific work gang out west of Baird in Eastland County. A contractor there offered to swap the stud for a mule Self owned. When you hauled dirt, as everybody knew, a good mule was worth two or three old studs. Nevertheless, Self allowed as how he would make the trade.

So now Self apparently figured he had a racehorse and there was even talk in the hotel saloon about a match race. Self was either the smartest or dumbest man around because he had mentioned matching his stud with Mayflower, Lee McCameron's quick little mare.

Hotel boss Brown Seay studied this for a time then called Chris Seale over and said, "Chris, better go out and look at this horse of Self's. See what you think of him."

Seale did just that. What he saw was a horse of fifteen hands, nicely "quartered" behind, well-balanced, yet certainly no show animal. The stud's head was a little common—but they didn't have halter contests in those days. Seale liked what he saw and as Seay came up to the saloon bar, Chris' report was to the point: "He can either not run a lick—or he's the fastest horse I ever saw."

The latter estimate soon proved correct. Self did arrange the match race with Mayflower, the race was run and one cowboy later remarked that Mayflower's rider couldn't have thrown a rock and hit the stud's dust. Within hours after that race, Triggerfoot Self and his horse were minor celebrities—and the horse was known by his name, Traveler.

Traveler was a good name for this animal. The most anybody could ever find out about him was that he came to Texas — maybe from New York — in a remuda of work animals. With other horses and mules, he pulled loads of dirt and earned his keep the first half of his life the hard way. Triggerfoot Self saw a little more to him than that. As shrewd judges of horseflesh, so did Brown Seay and Chris Seale . . . Didn't take either man long to decide they wanted to own, race and breed mares to that stallion. That's eventually what they did. Because they did, Traveler has become one of the immortals of the Quarter Horse breed as we know it now. "The Mystery Horse," as he's sometimes called, is regarded by many as the most important, prepotent sire in developing the modern Quarter breed. It has been estimated that roughly half of all the Quarter Horses alive today have Traveler someplace in their pedigrees.

It was Self who rescued the great animal from oblivion on the work dump. It was Seay and Seale who gave him first chance in the stud and it was oldtime horseman Ed Bateman of

Traveler is shown here in what would appear to be racing condition. Note the flecks of white on his coat. Turner Breedlove stands behind the horse, Grover Pruett holds the wiper, Clay Mann the halter.

Fort Worth who first chronicled in detail much of what we know today about Traveler. Bateman talked to many of the elderly cowboys who knew Traveler and his story in 1946 and wrote an account of it all for the fledgling Quarter Horse Association.

According to Bateman, Seay obtained ownership of Traveler after the stallion had won some tough match races against good short horses. It was horse-against-horse in those days, seventy years ago. No starting gates, no photo finishes — just a starting line, a starter and a finish line. But betting was heavy and a good horse race could bring out all the men — and most of the boys — in most Texas towns.

These two stallions are by Traveler, out of different mares. Their resemblance is apparent. At left is Possum, full brother to the noted Little Joe, out of the south Texas mare, Jenny. At right is Jack Tolliver, renamed Buster Brown, out of the Baird iceman's mare, Fanny Pace. Buster Brown was destined for fame as trick horse, polo pony and world traveler. Note the similarity in conformation, color and stance.

How Seay separated Self from Traveler is described by Bateman this way: Seay offered to run a horse named Froggie against Traveler and each man put up $500. If Traveler beat Froggie, Self was to win the $500 and get another $500 — but Self had to take Froggie while Seay took ownership of Traveler.

You've already guessed the outcome. Traveler won with ease and changed owners — and probably destinies as well. But the stallion's racing days weren't quite over yet. His new owner raced Traveler until he virtually raced him out of business. Across Central Texas Traveler answered every challenge and we have only one report of his ever losing — although match race records and times from those days almost don't exist now.

One of his toughest races was against the fine match racehorse, Bob Wilson. Traveler won by a nose—but Bob Wilson carried a 165-pound cowboy named Austin Merrick, reputed to be the only cowboy tough enough to ride Traveler's opponent. Traveler carried less weight than that.

So before retiring fulltime to breeding farm use, Traveler made his reputation as a running horse — and made it long after most stallions have any thought of running for their oats. Quarter Horsemen today, however, are more interested in the breeding aspects of the noted sire. Here is his lasting claim to fame. Veteran South Texas Breeder George Clegg once wrote about Traveler, "He was one of the most perfect looking horses I ever saw and sired great running horses from good mares."

In point of fact, Traveler did somewhat more than that. He sired *outstanding* horses from mares considered in that day to be ordinary at best. The most noted example of this is the trio of full brothers Traveler sired from Fanny Pace.

Fanny was a mare of unknown breeding. She helped her owner, Tump Pace, earn his living by pulling his ice wagon. Pace was the town's ice man and Fanny was a familiar sight in front of his vehicle. Fanny was bred to Traveler for three successive years — and produced horses named Judge Thomas, Judge Welch and Jack Tolliver (later renamed Buster Brown). Judge Thomas is said to have held the world's record at 770 yards for a quarter of a century after running that distance in 40.1 seconds at Butte, Montana, about 1902. Judge Welch also developed into an outstanding racehorse. However, he did not achieve the recognition of his brother since he was not campaigned extensively. Fanny Pace's youngest colt by Traveler became famous as Buster Brown and was regarded as an outstanding polo horse at maturity.

According to Miss Ella Moore Seale, daughter of Chris Seale, the darkest day of her childhood came when her father sold Buster Brown to a Virginia polo player named E. H. (Boogie) Leache. Leache took the stallion to Virginia where he was trained as a hunter, then later a trick horse in the first decade of the 20th century. But the decision to sell Jack Tolliver, nee Buster Brown, was a shattering one for the Seale household. Recalls Ella:

"He was foaled about 1902 or 1903, was a bright red sorrel

about 14.3... Fanny died when Jack was a colt... we came in from the lot and I was blubbering... 'Old Fanny is dead and Jack is a little orphan.' He grew up and had a 'patch' of his own with a little barn in it—for fifty years we called it the 'Jack Tolliver patch.' The entire family loved him. Somewhere around or before 1905 Leache somehow heard of him . . . he wired Chris from Boston an offer of $500 to ship the horse to Boston.

"I can faintly remember the debating that went on — of course Mama and the kids didn't want to sell but Chris, trying to pay for all the high-priced land we had bought (at $3.75 per acre), knew that $500 would help... (so) they led Jack with me aboard from his 'patch' to the front gate for the farewell... there was 'moaning at the bar'."

Renamed and schooled, Buster led a glamorous and active life. This Traveler son went to England, became a great polo horse, got wide publicity (In *Bit and Spur*, about 1908) and, according to Miss Seale, sired some fine offspring of his own.

On this point — the gender of Judge Welch, Judge Thomas and Buster Brown — there is little data to go on more than half a century later. Bateman and later writers say the three Traveler sons were gelded. Miss Seale, however, recalls a number of good sons and daughters of Buster Brown and Judge Welch. One fine Judge Welch son she remembers was The Virginian, a black stud that E. H. Leache bred from a noted polo mare, Little Sis. It is quite possible that most of Traveler's early colts were indeed gelded — but perhaps not until they had sired a number of sons and daughters. Ella Seale says that Judge Welch stayed on the place for some twelve years before he too went east. She is certain of having ridden good colts of his.

T his is also supported by one of the few men alive today who knew Traveler well, and his offspring: George Blakeley. He is now eighty-three years old and lives in retirement near Baird. His hearing isn't what it once was but his memory is clear on the horses that he knew and trained as a young cowboy in Baird sixty-five years ago. In an interview with this writer, Blakeley had these recollections:

"They drove him (Traveler) in here to a wagon with chain

harness on him. And they held some races here...and he out-ran everything. Chris Seale and Brown Seay bought him off this man...(paid) $100, that's what I heard them say. He (Traveler) was fifteen hands high and I imagine he'd weigh about 1,000 pounds. I think he was the best there ever was in this country. He was a chestnut sorrel and he had little white hairs scattered all over him.

"Judge Thomas, I've seen him, he was a great big horse, sixteen hands high, they sold him and he went 'way north somewhere. They kept Judge Welch here. I used to work him. I've plowed him and rode him...Mr. Seale had lots of land and lots of colts...he didn't raise many from old Traveler but he raised a lot of them from Judge Welch...I bet I broke thirty or forty colts by Judge Welch...

"They kept him (Traveler) here until he got old, they never did outrun him until Newman—lived at Sweetwater—outran him with a little mare. But he was getting old and all broke down. They never did outrun him until he was wore out. He was the best-dispositioned horse I ever saw—and nearly all his colts were that way, all easy-broke and all made good cow ponies . . ."

Nevertheless, it seems to be a fact that Traveler's offspring in the area where he was "discovered" don't loom as prominently in pedigree charts today as the later Traveler colts. It must be remembered that Traveler came along nearly half a century before the American Quarter Horse Association was founded. And without benefit of registration, many of the finest horses of that era never got the recognition they deserved.

Traveler is remembered partly because of horse historians like Ed Bateman, who chronicled the great stud's career in 1946 — and partly because of mares Traveler was to meet in the final years of his life.

After keeping the horse for some years, Chris Seale and Brown Seay sold Traveler to the Trammell family of Sweetwater, Texas, who in turn sold him to the Gardner Ranch of Big Lake. His final home was the ranch of the Shely brothers, Will and Dow, at Alfred, in South Texas. It was here that he died about 1910. Before he did, though, his colt crops became the talk of that arid, race-loving brush country. "Short horse" men of South Texas are a breed apart. This was especially true in the early days of the 20th century. To many a ranchman then, a matched horse race combined the emotional appeal of Mother, Home, Flag and Country. Small fortunes changed hands because of a man's pride — justified or not — in how quick his favorite horse could cover a quarter of a mile. And that distance is how the "Quarter" Horse got his name.

In the twilight of his life, at the Shely Ranch, Traveler got his best-known offspring. Bred to the great mare, Jenny, he sired Little Joe and Possum. Little Joe later was to sire Zantanon, the sire of King P-234. And as everybody knows who's ever been to a Quarter Horse show, King was—as Jess Hankins used to advertise him—a "cornerstone" of the breed. Little Joe also sired Joe Moore and that noted animal fathered another entire dynasty of fine running and working horses. Traveler also sired studs like Texas Chief and Joe Shely. In Ed Bateman's opinion, Texas Chief was Traveler's greatest colt. He had that early speed the cowmen wanted. He also had more size than most cow ponies of the time.

Little is known, unfortunately, of the many mares that bore the Traveler imprint, and how they fared when crossed on other noted strains of the period. There is George Clegg's letter to Bateman, saying in part: "I bought Texas Chief's mother and two of her fillies, one by Traveler and one by Rattler, an Adams horse. I bred them to Hickory Bill and raised one of the best studs this country ever saw from the old mare's filly by Traveler."

Men like Clegg, Ott Adams, Brown Seay, Chris Seale, all have passed on now and can't help us detail other Traveler offspring. Ella Moore Seale, who has probably ridden as many grandsons and granddaughters of Traveler as anyone alive today, still remembers their tractability and versatility. She raced them, worked cattle on them, jumped them through burning hoops, rode them down the road for pleasure.

Miss Seale still lives on the farm where she was born, where Fanny Pace pulled the ice wagon before she became a dam of champions — and where Traveler appeared — without benefit of pedigree or history, to help pave the way for a breed yet to come. ▲

15

ZANTANON

*"You call THAT a race horse?" the puzzled
visitor asked his Mexican friend.*

*"Well, senor, I have seen him run well, yes,"
replied the other man, smiling faintly.*

*"And you'll bet even money that the little horse
will win today?"*

*"Si, I make a small wager, senor — I would be
a poor host indeed if I did not permit you to select
whichever of the two horses that you judge most
worthy . . ."*

And so it was that another visitor to the Nuevo Laredo
section of Mexico wound up a sadder but wiser racing fan. The
horse that attracted his scorn certainly didn't *look* like a racehorse. Standing barely fourteen hands tall, the little stallion's
hip bones were clearly evident. So were his ribs. He stood in
the dusty street, in front of a saloon, shortly before time for
his owner to lead him to the nearby race course.

No doubt the dialogue above, or a reasonable facsimile,
was repeated many times over the years. The "little" horse
in question *was* a racehorse—although you might never sus-
pect it to look at him.

125

Many citizens of northern Mexico, however, knew all about this animal. Horse racing, although primitive in the 1920s, was almost a national pastime in parts of Mexico. *Aficionados* of the sport knew this stallion by name and reputation.

His name was Zantanon. His reputation: Unbeatable up to 300 yards, from a walking start. His nickname: The Man O'War of Mexico.

Racing records in those days were poorly kept. Stop watches clocked the times. So it is that we will never know precisely how great a racehorse Zantanon really was. Now it almost doesn't matter. The blood of this great animal made a contribution to today's Quarter Horses. He gave them speed and he gave them heart and the offspring he produced by many different mares insured his place among the great horses of the past.

Fortunately, the man who helped Zantanon achieve recognition as a sire—Manuel Benavides Volpe of Laredo, Texas— is very much alive and recalls some of the horse's races, then how he was plucked from obscurity.

Zantanon began life in auspicious surroundings. He was foaled on the Ott Adams ranch at Alice, Texas, March 28, 1917. That was the year the great Man O'War was foaled — thus Zantanon's comparison to the Thoroughbred horse. Zantanon's sire was the immortal Little Joe, which made him a half-brother to Joe Moore. His dam was Jeanette and Zantanon was clearly a superior colt, strong and quick. Nobody had to tell Ott Adams the colt had a future. But like many breeders today, Ott couldn't keep them all. And as a yearling the colt went across the border to Erasmo Flores of Nuevo Laredo. Later, Flores' uncle, Eutiquio, purchased the youngster, and raced him extensively . . . he was on the brush tracks of Mexico before he was two years old.

It is said that Zantanon's winnings were substantial, that he helped pay for a ranch and the buildings on it. Yet, according to M. Benavides Volpe, the little stallion was a great racehorse *despite* the way he was handled, not because of it.

"They didn't know how to feed him," Volpe says today. "He was nearly starved to death."

So it was that many a visitor to the towns of the region could scarcely believe that the dark chestnut stud was a cham-

Zantanon, shown at the age of four, is here ridden by Raynaldo Flores. He was usually tied to the horse by a surcingle. Volpe recalls Zantanon was in his best condition at time of this photo.

pion. Volpe related that his handlers would take him to the outskirts of a town and work him hard for several hours, then bring him into town and tie him up at the saloon — sometimes for half a day at a time. It was further related that Zantanon was walked some four miles on hard-surfaced streets to the race track for his workouts, then walked home over the same hard surface—where he was seldom cooled out but left tied under a tree during the heat of the day.

"By the day of the race," Volpe wrote some years ago, "he was so poor you could count each and every one of his ribs. By that time, of course, he had no pep and was absolutely dead on his feet. Yet in that condition, and with his owner's son weighing 140 pounds . . . he could run 300 yards in 15.4 seconds from a walking start."

It was clear, as many said, that Zantanon "won his races on his breeding only."

"I guess he was so poor," Volpe told one writer, "the horse knew he had to take every advantage—maybe it was his condition that made him smart. I've often wondered just what records Zantanon would have made had he been run under favorable conditions. I sincerely doubt there is a living horse today that could outrun Zantanon for 300 yards . . ."

In an article appearing in *The Quarter Horse* in 1948, Volpe recalls the last race he remembers seeing Zantanon run — against the fine mare Coneza.

"She was by Ace of Hearts and had beaten Pancho Villa in two different races. Pancho Villa, of course, was a full brother to Zantanon and many people believed that since the mare had twice defeated Pancho Villa, she could easily take Zantanon.

"Coneza came to the tracks ridden by a young man who was an excellent rider, but Zantanon was ridden by Calderon, an old and experienced jockey. The track was heavy and this was the advantage of Zantanon . . ."

In his prime, Zantanon was thick and powerful and his start was part of his success. So it was on the day of the race against Coneza that he put this blinding start to good use. At 300 yards one stride can mean victory — and as they jumped away, Zantanon had that stride.

". . . The little mare was simply out-generaled and outrun all the way," Volpe said.

One of the stories told in M. Volpe's family is how his father—one of Laredo's most distinguished citizens—developed a keen interest in finding a horse to beat Zantanon. The elder man had "learned to dislike the horse that had outrun him so many times."

In trying to beat him, Volpe's father bought a horse named Little Willie (also called The Swayback) from a rancher in Hallettsville, Texas. Zantanon was soon matched against the other and in the opinion of some, Zantanon had met his match. Little Willie was sired by Little Dick and had beat Pancho Villa in a match race.

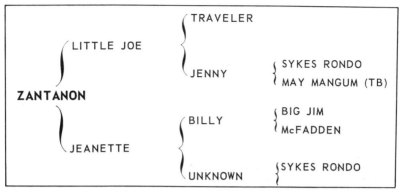

Came the day of the race and the two horses went to the
post. There was delay, then argument as one jockey complain-
ed that the other had many "tricks" at the start. On the rec-
ommendation of Zantanon's jockey, Calderon, the race was
not run.

It was a twist of fate when, some time later, the younger
Volpe purchased Zantanon — "and when I bought Zantanon my
father knew I had obtained one of the greatest old horses that
ever lived but he would never admit it."

It was no easy job to get Zantanon back to the United
States. Volpe was not able to buy the horse during the lifetime
of Don Eutiquio Flores. The purchase was made with his heirs
in 1931 — and the stallion, by then fourteen years old, cost
Volpe $500. This was considered an exorbitant price at the
time for a stud that old.

And in view of his condition, little wonder that some may
have thought Volpe unwise indeed! In his own words, the stallion was a pathetic sight.

"When we got him, he was starving to death . . . he was
covered in blue mud from one end to the other and full of ticks.
At the time, we didn't know what we had . . ."

It didn't take Zantanon long to demonstrate what Volpe had.
His offspring soon spoke for him. The list was long and today
constitutes a selection of royalty in the Quarter Horse breed.

Most noted of Zantanon's sons, of course, was King P-234.
This was to be probably the most famous sire of the Quarter
Horse breed. King was foaled on the Benavides Ranch near
Laredo, June 2, 1931. This was a decade before the establish-
ment of the American Quarter Horse Association, of course,
and his famous P-234 registration came many years later.

Zantanon, despite his rugged early years, lived to the age of twenty-four. Last surviving son of Zantanon was Ed Echols, a sire of both running and performance Quarter Horses.

Young King early demonstrated his sire's speed and it is said that Zantanon's noted son ran two races and won easily. He was then sold to Byrne James and trained for roping and cow work. He took to it readily—and in later years, as his get demonstrated this "cow," King blood became noted for stock-handling. From that time on, the King P-234 story became well known. Before his death at the age of twenty-five (on March 24, 1958) King sired 520 registered foals, including forty-six Register of Merit qualifiers—of which eleven earned AQHA Championships. An AQHA Championship was then the highest achievement in Quarter Horsedom. At the time of his death, King's stud fee was $2,500.

Among the great sires Zantanon produced, Ed Echols still lives, and has passed on the speed of his sire to many AAA and AA Register of Merit winners. His performance get too are noted—horses like Cherry Echols, Gin Echols, Cowboy Echols, Poco Diablo. San Siemon, out of Panita, was another of Zantanon's noted sons. Among his daughters was San Sue Darks, the dam of Leo San.

Zantanon also produced Zantanon, Jr., whose sons included AAA running horses and such sires as Red Gravey and Mr. Jimmy Hicks; Chico, who spread the Zantanon speed and strength to many Oklahoma breeding farms; El Bandido, who produced such offspring as Bandido's Gato and Bay Bandit; Little Potato, the fine broodmare who produced Dream Girl and Trace Plumas; and Shirley Temple, who as a two-year-old outran practically every good horse in south and west Texas.

Not to be overlooked also are such famous names as Cuatro de Julio, Zandy, Sonny Kimble, Cucuracha, Fourth of July, Lightning — all got speed and tremendous "bottom" from Zantanon.

Byrne James of Raymondville would testify to that. At one point in his later life, Zantanon was sold to James. But Volpe could not stand the horse being away from his place. He went to James and asked to buy him back. ". . . He wanted the horse so badly that I could not refuse to sell him," said James.

Of Zantanon, James says: "He was a good breeder and a great horse that never had a chance and yet proved himself to be one of the greatest sires of the Southwest, and one of the best short horses ever to step upon a track in northern Mexico."

Despite his early hardships, Zantanon had a long life, as horse longevity is measured. He got sick in 1941, when he was twenty-four years old, and was sent to the farm of the late Alonzo Taylor at Hebbronville, Texas. It was planned for him to be treated by the King Ranch veterinarian, Doctor J. K. Northway. But Zantanon died soon after his arrival.

Horses like this one, however, achieve their own particular immortality. Go to any Quarter Horse show or race meet in the Southwest and watch the horses and talk to their owners. Among the champions, many can be traced, both in pedigree as well as obvious ability, to the great Man O'War of Mexico. ▲

Other publications of

CORDOVAN CORPORATION

Horseman Magazine

The monthly Magazine of Western Riding is a lively informative guide to buying, training, enjoying and winning with a western horse. Each month there is news of Quarter Horse, Appaloosa, Pinto and other breed competitions, as well as news of open shows, cuttings, ropings, barrel races and rodeo. Features important "how to" articles by and with the nation's leading stock horse trainers plus tips on horse production and care from outstanding breeders. Subscription: 1 year $4, 2 years $6, 3 years $8.

Training Tips for Western Riders

Trainer-Judge L. N. Sikes and Horseman Editor Bob Gray have filled this inexpensive training manual with horse-country know-how. There are tips on early colt haltering, bits for young horses, hobbles, barrel racing techniques, cutting lessons and plain talk on training your horse to stop, back and lead properly. Also important suggestions on proper feeding procedures and preparing a horse for halter showing. $3.00.

Western Riding Games and Contests

Here is the long awaited book that tells you the rules and techniques for staging and competing in America's most popular stock saddle contests. In plain language with dramatic action photos, the book gives not only contest regulations, but important suggestions on horse training and handling for various competitions. Chapters cover cutting, roping, stake race, pole bending, barrel racing, baton relay, flag race, keyhole race, potato race, ring race, reining, rescue race, wagon race and prairie stump race. By Bob Gray $3.75.

Making Money With Western Horses

This book tells the important details about large and small horse breeding farms, horse sales of different kinds, preparing a horse for show and sale, stud care during the breeding season, marketing, showmanship—and many 'tips' that professional horsemen learn only from long experience. Author George Tyler is Quarter Horse judge, breeder, exhibitor and one of the nation's most successful "horse traders." If you raise horses for pleasure or profit this book can be one of the most important you ever read. $4.50.

Tips From Trainers

Here, in one inexpensive volume, are some of the outstanding "how-to" interviews printed in HORSEMAN between 1961 and 1965. Included are valuable training tips from such men as Buster Welch, Matlock Rose, Amye Gamblin, Jim Bob Altizer, Punch Oglesby, John Carter, Bubba Cascio, Lanham Riley, and Tom McNair. Subjects cover roping, reining, cutting, grooming, race training, colt handling and others vital to sound training and showing $1.50.

Championship Barrel Racing

The first comprehensive book on the country's exciting stock saddle sport, written by World Champion Barrel Racer Jane Mayo and Horseman Editor Bob Gray. With action photos, this book tells you essentials of recognizing a good barrel horse, starting a young one, barrel footwork, speed and its control—plus many hauling and contest tips that will help you win more often in competition. $4.00

Cordovan Corporation   Houston, Texas 77055